Mastering
Professional Scrum

Mastering Professional Scrum

A PRACTITIONER'S GUIDE TO OVERCOMING CHALLENGES AND MAXIMIZING THE BENEFITS OF AGILITY

Stephanie Ockerman

Simon Reindl

✦✦Addison-Wesley

Boston • Columbus • New York • San Francisco • Amsterdam • Cape Town
Dubai • London • Madrid • Milan • Munich • Paris • Montreal • Toronto • Delhi • Mexico City
São Paulo • Sydney • Hong Kong • Seoul • Singapore • Taipei • Tokyo

Visit us on the Web: informit.com/aw

Library of Congress Control Number: 2019945044

Copyright © 2020 Stephanie Ockerman and Simon Reindl

Cover design by Sabrina Love

Cover illustration by Maglyvi/Shutterstock

Cover art Maze licensed from mazegenerator.net

ISBN-13: 978-0-13-484152-6
ISBN-10: 0-13-484152-2

To the people who show up every day and do the hard work to create more inclusive, kind, and resilient organizations, communities, and societies. And to all of the women and allies who have empowered, inspired, and enabled me on my own leadership journey.
—Stephanie

To my wonderful family, without whose patience this would not have been possible. To my amazing, supportive, and loving wife, Sarah, and my two awesome children, Ella and George. Thank you for the joy and laughter and fresh perspective you bring to my world.
—Simon

CONTENTS

FOREWORD BY KEN SCHWABER

I created Scrum to improve the way in which I and others develop software. Scrum has been refined over the last 27 years, mostly through the creation, publishing, and gentle refinement of the Scrum Guide. Jeff Sutherland (the coauthor of Scrum) and I posted Scrum, as precisely defined in the Scrum Guide, online so people can suggest improvements. Over the years, we have refined Scrum based on these comments, making Scrum easier to use and understand.

When I first used the phrase "Scrum Master," many people became confused. Nobody was mastering Scrum; we were all learning how to use it and how to augment it with practices and tools so as to improve outcomes and to help team members use Scrum with proper values, practices, artifacts ("Done" Increments), and roles—all working together to achieve Scrum's goals.

The Scrum Master's job is to help the organization and the Scrum Team use Scrum properly to improve their ability to deliver value. The Scrum Master has to help the team members and people who are affected by Scrum (human resources, finance, etc.) understand how they can operate optimally. Anyone on the Scrum Team can improve their Scrum *mastery*; they can become better at using Scrum and empiricism to achieve better results, to deliver more value, in complex domains. Anyone can become *more professional.*

A professional is someone who works for money and follows the rules established for the profession. Professionals act and work according to standards, where they exist (e.g., adhering to the rules set forth in the Scrum Guide). They also embrace and embody a set of ethical principles established by their profession (e.g., the Scrum values of Focus, Commitment, Openness, Respect, and Courage).

Sometimes the Scrum professional may be torn between two alternatives. In these circumstances, the Agile Manifesto provides higher-level guidance:

- Individuals and interactions over processes and tools
- Working software over comprehensive documentation
- Customer collaboration over contract negotiation
- Responding to change over following a plan

Scrum professionals do not redefine Scrum itself or "tailor" it to their organizations; Scrum is Scrum. To create Increments of valuable Product and reach the desired outcomes, they *do* add supporting and ancillary practices, including DevOps, Kanban, and testing, reconciliation, and communication practices. Practices that distinguish Scrum from other approaches to complex work include the following:

1. The team organizes work in *short cycles.*
2. Management *doesn't interrupt* the team during a work cycle.
3. The team reports to *the client*, not to the manager.
4. The team estimates *how much time and effort* that work will take.
5. The team decides *how much* work it can do in an iteration.
6. The team decides *how* to do the iteration's work.
7. The team *measures its own performance.*
8. The team defines work goals *before* each cycle starts.

9. The team defines work and desired outcomes through a progressively refined description of outcomes (called the Product Backlog).

10. The team works to systematically and continuously improve and to remove impediments.

Our job as Scrum professionals is to continually improve our ability to use Scrum to deliver products and services that help customers achieve valuable outcomes. This book will help you to improve your ability to apply Scrum. Its authors share their experiences and advice, gathered from helping many clients and students learn and apply Scrum in their organizations. I hope that it helps you in your own professional journey.

Scrum on!

—*Ken Schwaber, co-creator of Scrum and founder of Scrum.org*

FOREWORD BY DAVE WEST

What is Professional Scrum?

There is no question that the world of work is becoming more complex. It's not that simple work is going away, but rather that much of this work will be replaced by automation, algorithms, and robotics. Complex work is best defined as work that is unknown—not just in terms of how we do it, but also in regard to the outcomes and impacts of that work. Even when we have a clear outcome in mind, it is only after we have delivered something that we appreciate that the impact of the change may be different from the one we intended.

Scrum was developed to help us chart our way through a complex world. The framework is simple yet powerful, providing a way to bring order and structure to complexity through discovery and learning. But to be effective with Scrum requires something more than just following the mechanics of the framework: It requires a professional attitude.

Ken Schwaber, the co-creator of Scrum, describes a *professional* as someone who works for money and follows established rules for the profession. He also adds that to be a professional means embracing a set of ethical standards. These standards both unify members of a profession and define that profession to the outside world, as does the Hippocratic Oath for the medical profession.

Building upon that model of professionalism, four additional elements are key to achieving professionalism using the Scrum Framework:

- **Discipline.** To be effective with Scrum requires discipline. You have to deliver to gain learning; you have to do the mechanics of Scrum; you have to challenge your preconceived ideas about your skills, role, and understanding of the problem; and you have to work in a transparent and structured way. Discipline is hard and may at times seem unfair as your work exposes problem after problem and your efforts seem in vain.

- **Behaviors.** The Scrum Values were introduced in the Scrum Guide in 2016 in response to the need for a supporting culture that would enable Scrum to be successful. The Scrum Values describe five simple ideas that when practiced encourage an agile culture: Courage, Focus, Commitment, Respect, and Openness describe behaviors that both Scrum Teams and the organizations they work within should exhibit.

- **Value.** Scrum Teams work on problems that, when solved, deliver value to customers and stakeholders. Teams work for a customer who rewards them for that work. But the relationship is complex, because the problems are complex: Customers might not know what they want, or the economics of the solution might be unclear, or the quality and safety of the solution may be unknown. The job of a Professional Scrum Team is, to the best of their ability, to do the right thing for all these parties by delivering a solution that best meets their customers' needs within the constraints that have been placed on them. That requires transparency, respect for each other and for customers, and a healthy dose of curiosity to uncover the truth.

- **Helping others.** Scrum is a team sport, but one where each team is small. In consequence, the team is often the underdog trying to solve problems that it barely has the skills and experience to solve. To be effective, Professional Scrum Teams must work with other members of their community to learn new skills and share experiences. Helping to scale the agility of the community is not completely altruistic, because the helpers often learn valuable things that they can bring back to help their own teams. Professional Scrum encourages people to form professional networks in which ideas and experiences that help teams can be exchanged.

Merely describing Professional Scrum does very little to help you realize those ideas in your organization or on your product. That is where Stephanie and Simon's book comes in: It is a support book for Professional Scrum. It takes the Core Scrum Framework and puts it in the context of professionalism, describing why many of these ideas make sense and how they have evolved from different disciplines and concepts. Whether you read it from cover to cover or dip into a particular section for specific guidance, it provides practical advice for how you can master Scrum and become more professional. And that journey is long and never ends.

Good luck, and enjoy the ride.

—Dave West, CEO and Product Owner Scrum.org

INTRODUCTION

We live in a world in which the only certainty is uncertainty. As the world becomes more interconnected and interdependent, it also becomes more complex. And it's changing rapidly: New customers and competitors can appear, evolve, and disappear before we have a chance to respond. Technology is constantly changing, new political realities can create new regulatory and legal requirements to meet, and malicious hackers seem to learn faster than our ability to thwart them.

In response to this uncertainty, we accept the fact that we cannot predict the future. The best we can do is to act intentionally, taking small steps forward, embracing uncertainty, embracing empiricism, and using feedback loops to learn. This is the heart of agility and the foundation of Scrum: planning in small increments, delivering a working Product Increment, inspecting the result, and adapting, repeatedly and with complete transparency. But for agility to work, it must be pursued with professionalism.

Evidence of a lack of professionalism is everywhere: from the order that arrives with the wrong items, to the phone app that won't work, to the reports of security breaches that expose our private information to unauthorized parties. It manifests itself in projects that spiral out of control, costing millions of dollars while delivering nothing of value. It also manifests itself in personal terms: valuable working years wasted without developing new skills or opening up new opportunities. It undermines trust and damages working relationships. Anyone who has worked in product development has experienced at least some of its symptoms:

- Lack of transparency with respect to progress, quality, and outcomes
- Promising false certainty and avoiding open and honest conversations about complexity and risk
- Cutting quality to save money or time
- Avoiding accountability
- Delivering products that do not achieve acceptable quality so as to hit a delivery date
- Ignoring new information and carrying on with the plan

SCRUM PROVIDES A WAY FORWARD, IF PURSUED WITH PROFESSIONALISM

Scrum is an empirical approach to delivering products in a complex and uncertain world. While Scrum is widely adopted, a lot of it is not very professional. As Scrum co-founder Ken Schwaber observes, "Scrum is simple to understand, yet difficult to master."[1] Among the various teams and organizations that are actually doing Scrum, many are simply going through the motions. We call this "mechanical Scrum." Such teams use Scrum terminology without understanding the intent behind it or exhibiting the discipline that Scrum requires.

This book aims to dispel the myths, correct misunderstandings, and help organizations to use Scrum to deliver high-quality products and experiences for their customers. In short, it aims to help organizations apply Scrum while achieving professionalism.

---

1. www.scrumguides.com

WHO SHOULD READ THIS BOOK

This book is intended for people who have a working knowledge of Scrum, who may be doing many things right but want to improve. You may be a Scrum Master, but you could also be a Development Team member or a Product Owner. The important thing is that you want to, and need to, improve. If you want to learn about Scrum, we suggest you start with the Scrum Guide, a class about Scrum, or one of the many excellent introductory books on the subject.[2]

HOW THIS BOOK IS ORGANIZED

Our intent in writing this book was to provide you with a virtual Scrum Coach to assist you on your journey, helping you face challenges with transparency and courage, and introducing you to new approaches that will help you to master Scrum, exhibit professionalism, and enable business agility. We don't have all the answers, but we will provide tools that you can use to find your own answers to your unique challenges.

To simplify the journey toward Scrum mastery, we have designed an approach for Professional Scrum that synthesizes what we have learned and provides a compass to help you navigate during your own journey. This approach is based on our experience as practitioners, Professional Scrum Trainers, and our learnings from the wider Scrum.org community. Where you start on your journey is up to you.

Each chapter focuses on a particular set of challenges:

- **Chapter 1: Continuously Improving Your Scrum Practice** provides a way of taking stock of your current practices, supported by the self-assessment in Appendix A, with an eye toward identifying areas for improvement.

---

2. To find a class, see https://www.scrum.org/courses. If you're looking for a concise book about Scrum, we recommend *Scrum: A Pocket Guide* by Gunther Verheyen (Van Haren Publishing, 2013).

- **Chapter 2: Creating a Strong Team Foundation** helps you understand how your team works together, identify areas for improvement, and use appropriate techniques to improve the team's composition and way of working.

- **Chapter 3: Delivering "Done" Product Increments** explains why "Done" is the most critical concept in Scrum and why "undone" work is a sign that something is terribly wrong and needs to be fixed.

- **Chapter 4: Improving Value Delivered** focuses on measuring the value delivered by your "Done" Product Increment and provides practices to improve the value you deliver over time.

- **Chapter 5: Improving Planning** helps you improve the way that you decide what work you're going to do and focus on delivering high-value Product Increments while eliminating "undone" work.

- **Chapter 6: Helping Scrum Teams Develop and Improve** reveals the barriers that a team might face in delivering "Done" Product Increments and suggests strategies to overcome them.

- **Chapter 7: Leveraging the Organization to Improve** considers how organizational impediments can limit a team's ability to deliver and addresses what you can do to overcome those obstacles.

- **Chapter 8: Conclusion and What's Next** provides a look back at the journey you've been on in this book and suggests some ways to continue your journey.

- **Appendix A: A Self-Assessment for Understanding Where You Are** provides a means for assessing your current Scrum practices.

- **Appendix B: Common Misconceptions About Scrum** describes and corrects common misunderstandings about what Scrum is and what it isn't.

CALL TO ACTION

As you continue forward, we encourage you to start some powerful and productive conversations, which will help you get the most out of this book. First, you should reflect on where you are now and where you want to go.

Remember to ask for different perspectives while identifying common goals. Here are some questions to get you started:

1. What does business agility mean to our organization? How does that relate to our mission? What benefits do we expect to see as an organization? What will it look like when we achieve our vision for agility? How will it feel different?

2. What does business agility mean to our team? What benefits do we expect to see? Which data can we use to understand agility at the team level and product level?

3. How does business agility relate to the product vision?

4. How soon can we get a return on investment (ROI)? What more do we want?

5. How much flexibility and control does our business have in making investment decisions? What more is needed?

6. How quickly can we take advantage of opportunities and respond to risks? What more do we want?

7. How do we demonstrate professionalism as a team? How do the organization's values and behaviors relate to professionalism?

8. What are some examples of unprofessional behavior that we have seen (or participated in) within our organization?

Register your copy of *Mastering Professional Scrum* on the InformIT site for convenient access to updates and/or corrections as they become available. To start the registration process, go to informit. com/register and log in or create an account. Enter the product ISBN (9780134841526) and click Submit. Look on the Registered Products tab for an Access Bonus Content link next to this product, and follow that link to access any available bonus materials. If you would like to be notified of exclusive offers on new editions and updates, please check the box to receive email from us.

ACKNOWLEDGMENTS

We had a lot of help and support in writing this book. First, we must thank Dave West, Kurt Bittner, and Ken Schwaber for their trust, support, encouragement, and perspective on what felt like an almost impossible challenge—writing a book that illuminates the power of Scrum, providing practical guidance, and moving people toward discovering their own Scrum mastery journey. Kurt Bittner performed the magic necessary to help us express our ideas more simply and effectively. Of course, we have to thank Ken Schwaber and Jeff Sutherland for creating Scrum itself, which has given us paths to fulfilling work that aligns with our values and purpose.

We have so much gratitude for the Professional Scrum Trainer community, whose members have supported us in our growth as product delivery practitioners, Professional Scrum Trainers, and entrepreneurs. Their generosity in sharing knowledge and experience, their commitment to learning and growth, and their willingness to show up fully make us grateful to be part of this community every single day.

Many individuals have inspired and challenged us in our personal Scrum mastery journeys. Our deepest gratitude goes to Todd Greene, Richard Hundhausen, Stacy Martin, Don McGreal, Steve Porter, Ryan Ripley, Steve Trapps, and many, many more.

—Simon and Stephanie

About the Authors

Stephanie Ockerman is the founder of Agile Socks LLC, an agile training and coaching business whose mission is to help people build amazing things together, so we can all thrive in an unpredictable and complex world. She brings more than 15 years of experience supporting teams and organizations in delivering valuable products and services, as a Scrum Master, as a trainer, as a coach, and as an organizational change agent. She also enjoys writing, speaking, photography, and traveling the world. You can read her blog and see what she is up to at AgileSocks.com.

Simon Reindl is focused on enabling individuals, teams, and organizations to optimize the delivery of value in a humane way. He has more than 25 years of experience developing and supporting products in a range of roles and a variety of industries around the world. Simon has worked in all of the Scrum roles and has supported organizations from start-ups to multinational corporations in harnessing empiricism. Simon was the first Professional Scrum

Trainer in the United Kingdom. He has trained thousands of people around the world, in government departments, private companies, and universities. When not running his company Advanced Product Delivery, he enjoys time with his family and scuba diving.

Both Stephanie and Simon are certified Professional Scrum Trainers (PSTs) and Stewards for the Professional Scrum Master (PSM) course taught around the world.

CONTINUOUSLY IMPROVING YOUR SCRUM PRACTICE

Scrum is a lightweight framework that helps teams create valuable releasable products frequently. The rules that exist for Scrum practice are important to ensure transparency, to enable effective inspecting and adapting, to reduce waste, and to enable business agility.[1]

No matter how experienced, every team can improve its ability to inspect and adapt to deliver valuable Product Increments. Customers are continually evolving, and their needs are constantly changing. Competitors are continually evolving and adapting as well. Likewise, technologies are constantly changing, enabling new capabilities while also creating new challenges to overcome. New team members bring new skills and insights but may change the dynamics of the team. Meeting these challenges means not only mastering the delivery of great products by using empiricism, but also inspecting, adapting, and improving the Scrum Team's capabilities.

---

1. To learn more about Scrum, see https://www.scrum.org/resources/what-is-scrum.

FOCUS ON SEVEN KEY AREAS TO IMPROVE YOUR SCRUM PRACTICE

To help you and your teams improve, we have broken the problem down into seven key improvements:

- An agile mindset
- Empiricism
- Teamwork
- Team process
- Team identity
- Product value
- Organization

AN AGILE MINDSET

An agile mindset is essential to improving the attitudes and outlooks held by the members of a Scrum Team, shaping how they interpret the world and how they work with each other and the world at large. When we talk about an agile mindset, we include the Scrum values,[2] the values and principles from the *Manifesto for Agile Software Development*,[3] and Lean Principles.[4] These values and principles guide the decisions that a Scrum Team makes, and they directly affect the effectiveness of that team in collaborating while using an empirical process to deliver valuable Product Increments.

Delivering value in a complex world means that there are few rules and no "best practices" that a team can apply. Instead, team members are guided by an agile mindset to make decisions based on the best data available to them.

---

2. www.scrumguides.org

3. agilemanifesto.org

4. See Mary Poppendieck and Tom Poppendieck, *Lean Software Development: An Agile Toolkit* (Boston: Addison-Wesley, 2003).

EMPIRICISM IS AT THE HEART OF SCRUM

Scrum is designed to enable empiricism. Embracing empiricism improves transparency, inspection, and adaptation. Understanding these three pillars of any empirical process is essential for a Scrum Team to improve its ability to deliver valuable Product Increments.

- **Transparency** means that the Scrum Team has a full understanding of what's going on; all aspects of the process that affect outcomes are visible to them. Transparency helps them understand which features and functions are planned for the product, how the Scrum Team is progressing toward its goals, and what value customers receive when they use the product.
- **Inspection** means that the Scrum Team is able, at frequent intervals, to observe results and learn from new information. Team members actively seek information about both achievements and shortfalls from desired outcomes and goals.
- **Adaptation** means that the Scrum Team, at frequent intervals, uses information obtained from inspection to change its strategy, plans, techniques, and behaviors to realign them with the desired outcomes and goals.

The Scrum Framework provides a set of lightweight rules that help a Scrum Team to achieve a minimal level of empiricism:

- Time-boxes help a Scrum Team create empirical feedback loops.
- By producing a "Done" Increment at least once during a Sprint, a Scrum Team enables transparency that allows them to validate their assumptions about value.

To truly maximize the benefits of Scrum, Scrum Teams must increase the breadth (quantity) and depth (quality) of their empiricism. For example:

- By increasing transparency into how they do their work, they are able to identify improvements in their processes, tools, and interactions.

- By increasing transparency into the value that customers realize from using the product, they gain deeper insights into how they can improve the product.

- By increasing their frequency of collaboration during the day, beyond just the Daily Scrum, they can identify and resolve issues sooner, thereby improving their flow of work.

- By collaborating with the Product Owner as the work is being done, they can increase the speed with which they are able to improve the product.

MASTERING SCRUM MEANS IMPROVING TEAMWORK

To make empiricism work, Scrum Teams need to collaborate to deliver valuable solutions to complex problems, then measure the results, and subsequently adapt based on feedback. An effective Scrum Team is:

- *Cross-functional.* A cross-functional team has all of the skills needed to accomplish the goal. This reduces the risk caused by dependencies outside the team, including potential waste from partially done work. "Cross-functional" does not mean that every person needs to be able to perform every activity. Instead, a team must figure out the combination of skills and how to spread the skills among the team to reduce waste, improve innovation and quality, and adapt to changing needs.

- *Self-organizing.* A self-organizing team determines what it can accomplish and how team members will work together to accomplish it. To ensure accountability, the first step is for a team to feel ownership of the work. Members need to be trusted as the experts and allowed to experiment, try new things, and change direction—all in the service of value delivery.

- *Collaborative.* To harness the power of collective intelligence, a self-organizing, cross-functional team must break down silos to gain the benefits of collaboration. Working in silos makes it challenging to innovate or even to simply deliver something of value to a customer quickly. Handoffs create gaps in understanding, delays, and other waste.

- *Stable.* A self-organizing, cross-functional, collaborative team is more than a collection of individuals; it is an entirely new entity made up of people who themselves are wonderfully complex creatures. It takes time and conscious effort to bring a group of individuals together to form a cohesive team that is able to continuously evolve in terms of who it is and how it works. Without stability, the team never completely forms, and its sponsoring organization never truly reaps the benefits of a high-performing team. This does not mean that team composition should never change, only that when it does it will take time and conscious effort to help the individuals work as a team again.

EVERY SCRUM TEAM MUST FOCUS ON IMPROVING THE VALUE THAT ITS PRODUCT DELIVERS

The purpose of a Scrum Team is to deliver a series of valuable Product Increments. To deliver value, a Scrum Team must:

• Understand the motivations, behaviors, and needs (both stated and latent) of users and customers.
• Align the product's vision, its strategy, and the mission and objectives of the organization.
• Measure the actual value delivered.

Essentially, Scrum enables a team to deliver a lot of stuff, frequently. However, if the team isn't optimizing the value of the Product, it will achieve very little.

EVERY STRONG TEAM HAS A DISTINCT TEAM IDENTITY

A team starts as a collection of individuals. Together they form an entirely new living and breathing organism. This new organism forms an identity over time. Just as a child grows up and becomes a teenager and then a young adult, a team must constantly seek to discover and evolve its identity.

At a fundamental level, establishing identity is about answering three big questions that guide a team on its journey toward high performance:

1. Why do we exist? (Purpose)
2. What is important to us? (Values)
3. What do we want? (Vision)

TO IMPROVE, TEAMS MUST HONE THEIR TEAM PROCESSES

The Scrum Team defines its way of working within *guard rails* established by the Scrum Framework—that is, the boundaries and guidance established by role accountabilities, event goals, and artifact purposes. How the Scrum Team fulfills the roles, uses the artifacts, and conducts the events is left up to them. How they create the Product Increment and ensure quality is also left up to them.

The Team Process dimension includes practices, tools, and ways of working together. It touches on a wide variety of areas, including the following:

- Engineering practices and tools
- Quality practices and tools
- Product management practices and tools
- Product Backlog management practices and tools
- Effective use of Scrum events and artifacts
- Effective communication and collaboration
- Identification and removal of sources of waste
- Identification and removal of impediments
- Effective use and growth of team knowledge, skills, and capabilities

The practices and tools that a team uses will be influenced by the product type, its technology platform, the environment in which the product is used, the users of the product and how they use it, regulatory and legal conditions, market trends, changing needs of the business, and so forth. That's a lot of stuff! Moreover, much of that stuff changes over time.

As a result, Scrum Teams must remain vigilant in inspecting and adapting what they are doing, why they are doing it, how they are doing it, and what benefits they are getting from doing it. New practices and tools are continuously being created and shared in product development communities around the world, so it is important to stay connected and keep learning. In fact, teams may need to invent new practices and tools to meet their unique challenges and needs.

THE ORGANIZATION CAN GREATLY INFLUENCE THE TEAM'S PERFORMANCE

Organizations provide both structure and culture. Both of these facets impact the teams and products that live within the organization, in either positive ways or negative ways.

Structure includes the business model, which is essentially the design for successfully operating the business. This includes the mission, the strategy, products, and services, as well as how they relate to revenue sources, a customer base, and financing. Structure also includes how employees, partners, and service providers are organized. It often influences organizational processes and policies.

Culture is a body of habits that bind people together into a cohesive unit. Culture is a way of seeing things, of knowing what to do in specific circumstances. It evolves from the sum of all human behavior within an organization. It is often influenced by the organizational structure and processes, including roles, goals, and incentives.

The success of Scrum Teams is greatly influenced by organizational structure and culture.

Maximizing the benefits of Scrum often means evolving organizational culture, processes, and possibly structure. Although you may not have to tackle these things immediately, usually Scrum Teams eventually start running into impediments that are outside of their control. They may be able to work around those impediments for a time, but this means they will reach a plateau.

GROWING SCRUM REQUIRES A TEAM TO IMPROVE OTHER CAPABILITIES

Scrum Teams need a number of capabilities to help them to continuously improve and to adapt to change. By "capability," we mean the ability to apply knowledge, skills, and experience to solve problems. Specifically, Scrum Teams must have knowledge (e.g., theory, techniques, domains), the ability to apply that knowledge skillfully to obtain desired results, and experience to build those skills as well as to guide intuition and foresight.

Scrum Teams need different capabilities depending on the kind of product they are developing and the constraints of the organization in which they work. The kinds of capabilities they need can be organized into five categories:

- Teaching skills
- Facilitation skills
- Coaching skills
- Technical excellence
- Servant leadership

People within the Scrum Team must have these capabilities and continue to grow these capabilities so as to be successful in the dimensions that enable Professional Scrum.

TEACHING SKILLS

Teaching is instructing others in an effort to give them new knowledge and skills. Often, Scrum Masters employ their teaching skills to help team members understand the Scrum Framework and its underlying values and principles. Scrum Teams will likely need to be introduced to techniques that can help them move forward with Scrum and become more effective with Scrum.

The skills and knowledge that a Scrum Team needs to continuously improve and tackle new challenges will change over time. Scrum Masters recognize what the Scrum Team needs based on its growth as a team and the current context to help the team get to the next level needed. This may be professional training, short exercises and knowledge sharing, a refresher course, a situational teaching moment, or a combination of all of these.

Of course, it is not always the Scrum Master who needs to teach the team. Product Owners may teach Development Teams about the product market, customer needs, and business value. Development Team members may teach each other about quality practices, testing approaches, and tools.

Teaching does not simply mean telling people things; that is, teaching is not a lecture. People learn much more effectively by doing and discovering. They learn by relating to what they already know. They also learn when the new knowledge and skills have an emotional impact.

Teaching is not something everyone can do. Some people may have an innate teaching ability, but ultimately teaching is a capability that people can develop and grow. Luckily, you do not have to be at the level of a professional teacher to employ and develop this capability.

Facilitation Skills

Facilitators guide groups by using a neutral perspective to help them come to their own solutions and make decisions. The facilitator provides a group with enough structure to enable the members to engage in positive collaboration to achieve productive progress in meetings and conversations. The word "facile" is French for "easy" or "simple"; thus, a facilitator is trying to make things easier for a group of people to work together.

Facilitation skills can help improve every Scrum event. In addition, facilitation can help improve other working sessions as well as ad hoc conversations that occur when teams are doing complex work together.

The extent of facilitation can range from light to extensive, depending on the needs of the group. Wherever a meeting or conversation falls on this range, ensure there is enough structure to meet the following aims:

- Stay on target with their purpose or goals.
- Create an environment that promotes rich discussion and collaboration.
- Clarify the group's decisions, key outcomes, and next steps.

Any team member can help the team by facilitating. The Scrum Guide does not require the Scrum Master to facilitate all of the events; instead, facilitation is a skill that can and should be grown across a Scrum Team. Facilitation skills also help team members guide their own informal conversations and working sessions with each other to be more focused, creative, and productive.

Coaching Skills

Coaching enhances a person's ability to learn, make changes, and achieve desired goals. It is a thought-provoking and creative process that enables people to make conscious decisions and empowers them to become leaders in their own lives.[5]

Our view is that coaching is *not* the same as advising or consulting. The key difference is that the person being coached is the one taking the lead. With advising, the person being advised is not learning and discovering based on his or her own experiences and desires, but rather receives advice based on someone else's experience and desires. "Consulting" is a broad and loosely used term, but it typically involves doing the work (versus helping others discover solutions) and advising people how to do the work.

Coaching skills help Scrum Teams grow because they help the team members improve their accountability and ability to self-organize. They also help the team become more resilient when faced with complexity, new challenges, and constant change.

Technical Excellence

Technical excellence means excellence in the choice and application of techniques; it is not just about the technology. Scrum doesn't tell you how to be an excellent Development Team, nor does it tell you how to be an excellent Product Owner. The approaches, skills, and tools you will need in each role are completely dependent on the context in which you are working. Although Scrum doesn't define what sort of things you will need to exhibit technical

---

5. For even more information on coaching, see the International Coach Federation (https://coachfederation.org/) and the Coach Training Institute (https://coactive.com/).

excellence, doing Scrum well absolutely requires that you demonstrate technical excellence. Technical excellence encompasses many things: from engineering practices to programming languages, from product management practices to quality assurance, from mechanical engineering to user experience design, and much more.

Because technology and business are changing so rapidly, along with other environmental changes that impact product possibilities, any attempt to define exactly what is needed to deliver with technical excellence would become outdated immediately. Furthermore, products are becoming much more than just software. As a result, Scrum Teams need to constantly refine and evolve what technical excellence means to them as business and technology needs change.

SERVANT LEADERSHIP

The Scrum Guide describes the Scrum Master as a servant-leader and provides examples of ways that the Scrum Master serves the Product Owner, the Development Team, and the organization. Scrum Masters are accountable servant-leaders, which means a Scrum Master's success is determined by the success of his or her Scrum Team. A Scrum Master helps everyone grow their capabilities, effectively navigate limitations and challenges, and embrace empiricism to deliver, on a frequent cadence, valuable products in a complex and unpredictable world.

However, there is an artful complexity to fulfilling the accountability of the Scrum Master role. When success depends on the actions of others, it is easy to want to direct them and step in when things appear to be going off-course. Yet such intervention can undermine self-organization and their feeling of accountability. This is where the capabilities of servant leadership guide a Scrum Master.

Here are examples of behaviors of accountable Scrum Masters:

- They create an environment of safety, encouraging productive debate to ensure people feel heard and respected, thereby helping teams reach better decisions and own those decisions.
- They facilitate consensus, helping teams clarify decisions and responsibilities to increase focus and create shared understanding.
- They refrain from solving problems and aim to increase transparency, which empowers teams and helps them to better self-organize, taking ownership of their process, decisions, and outcomes.
- They are comfortable with failure and ambiguity. When team decisions do not lead to the anticipated outcome, they help the team learn and grow and gain confidence in using an empirical approach that maximizes learning and controls risk.
- They care for people, meeting them where they are and helping them find their next step for growth, but are not afraid to challenge people when they are capable of more.
- They show low tolerance for organizational impediments and fiercely advocate for the team to remove obstacles that are preventing the team from achieving better results.

These behaviors contribute to higher engagement, faster feedback, and better outcomes for the product. When managers of Scrum Teams and other leaders in the organization act as accountable servant-leaders, they support the growth of both Scrum Teams and agility across the wider organization.[6]

A Process for Continuous Improvement

Appendix A, "A Self-Assessment for Understanding Where You Are," presents a set of self-assessment questions. If you take the time with your team members to complete this assessment, it will bring additional perspectives and insights. The assessment is meant to help you identify areas where you

---

6. You can learn more about servant leadership in the context of Scrum from Geoff Watts' *Scrum Mastery* (Inspect & Adapt Ltd., 2013).

can improve as a team; it is not meant to pass judgment on you for doing things wrong. Ideally, this tool will prompt your entire Scrum Team to look objectively at where you are and where you want to be, as a starting point for your team's improvement.

After you have completed the self-assessment, look for questions where you scored yourself as 7 or lower. Especially look at questions where you scored yourself as 5 or lower.

The list of areas where you feel you need to improve may feel overwhelming, but as we said earlier, transparency is essential to improving the results that you will get by using Scrum. The way you start improving anything complex is to ask yourself three questions:

1. What hurts the most?
2. Why?
3. What are small experiments we can run that will deliver the most value?

What Hurts the Most?

You can't fix everything at once. Your energy and focus will become diluted when you try to change too many things simultaneously, making it difficult to achieve anything meaningful for any one thing. When people in the organization don't see quick benefits, they tend to lose interest and withdraw their support, and the new habits may not be given the chance to take hold. Spreading yourself across too many things also makes it difficult to measure the impacts of each change or to know which changes are having the desired impacts.

Instead, incrementally implement changes continuously over time, making adjustments as you learn more—in other words, improve empirically! Sometimes the changes will be small, and sometimes the changes must be big. It all depends on what is broken. The best place to start is usually where it hurts the most.

In Practice: Seven Common Scrum Dysfunctions

In our experience, seven common mistakes prevent teams and organizations from fully enabling business agility with Professional Scrum. These mistakes can happen even with the best of intentions.

1. **Undone Scrum.** In our experience with a wide variety of teams, we have found that the biggest pain point for Scrum Teams is not being able to create a "Done" Product Increment by the end of a Sprint. Scrum Teams that don't produce a "Done" Increment can't inspect and adapt and are not really getting any benefit from using Scrum. This can lead to "zombie" Scrum, or water-Scrum-fall, or several of the other dysfunctions listed here.

2. **Mechanical (or Zombie) Scrum.** This problem involves simply going through the motions without the spirit of continuous improvement and without understanding or caring about the underlying values and principles. This is "checking the box" to say you are doing it, but there's no beating heart.

3. **Dogmatic Scrum.** This issue may happen when an "expert" tells the Scrum Team the "best practices" based on his or her own experience. *There are no best practices with Scrum.* The assertion that teams must follow certain "best practices" discourages self-organization and ultimately limits agility. Scrum is meant to be a framework for opportunistic discovery.

   The reason Scrum is so lightweight is because specific practices and techniques are not universal. Product delivery is complex and unpredictable, and it requires creative exploration by self-organizing teams. The best practice is the practice that works for your product and your team in the current moment. And it likely won't be a best practice for your product and your team six months from now.

4. **One-Size-Fits-All Scrum.** In one-size-fits-all Scrum, an organization wants to standardize and create a Scrum "methodology" for all Scrum Teams in the organization. This problem, which is often combined with dogmatic Scrum, sometimes emerges more because of a (misplaced) feeling of control and predictability, rather than out of a sense of creating true value for the organization. It may represent an attempt to ensure all previous activities and documents are "covered."

   In Scrum, the activities are not what matter; the outcomes are what matter. We need to be open to new ways of working to meet the real needs. Scrum is a process framework, and teams need to figure out their own process within the boundaries of Scrum.

5. **Water-Scrum-Fall.** This problem comes in two flavors. In the first version, a Scrum Team is operating in a series of Sprints but essentially still doing a waterfall process within the Sprint, with silos of knowledge and skills and multiple handoffs. This often results in not having a "Done" Increment by the end of the Sprint.

   In the second manifestation, a Scrum Team does its "development" work in a Sprint, but there are up-front requirements and design cycles and later testing cycles. This is not really Scrum at all, because there is no intention of producing a releasable Increment at the end of every Sprint.

6. **Good Enough Scrum.** With this problem, the Scrum Team gets some efficiency benefits by regularly planning and looking at the state of the product, but it tolerates the organizational impediments and current limitations, assuming "that's the way things have always been done." Team members don't challenge themselves to improve technical and engineering practices to have a "Done" Increment every Sprint.

7. **Snowflake Scrum.** This situation happens when a team or organization thinks it is "unique," so it has to adapt Scrum to fit its needs. *You either do Scrum or you don't do Scrum.* Modifying Scrum does not fix the problems. Modifying Scrum will likely hide your problems ... for a little while. When the problems are hidden, it may feel better—but those problems are still there. Ultimately, they will manifest as a lack of business agility and dysfunction.

ROOT CAUSE ANALYSIS

The question "why" is about getting down to the root cause. The *5 Whys* is a technique used to determine the root cause of a problem by repeating the question "Why."[7] The "5" in the name of this technique comes from observation that typically five iterations of asking the question are needed to get to the root of the problem, although the actual number may be either fewer or more.

---

7. For more information about the "5 Whys" technique, see https://link.springer.com/chapter/10.1007%2F978-981-10-0983-9_32.

In Practice: Using the "5 Whys" to Diagnose Root Causes

To illustrate using the 5 Whys, consider the following problem: "Releases are constantly delayed, frustrating customers and other stakeholders."

The first question you could ask is "Why are releases constantly delayed?" Your answer might be "Because we didn't deliver a 'Done' Product Increment, so our work has to continue into the next Sprint."

In response, your second question would likely be "Why didn't you deliver a 'Done' Product Increment?" Your answer might be "Product Backlog items are always larger and more difficult than we think, and we don't usually discover this until late in the Sprint."

Based on your experience you may already have thought of some possible root causes:

- The work is too big. (Team Process)

- The work is not well enough understood. (Team Process, Product Value)

- How the team gets things to "Done" is not transparent or not effective. (Empiricism, Teamwork, Team Process)

- Progress is not transparent. (Empiricism, Team Process)

- Team members may be afraid to bring up issues and risks. (Teamwork, Team Identity)

You can now form better questions to start digging deeper into the root causes. Your third question might be "How much transparency is there to the progress of work on a daily basis?" The answer might be "We have a Daily Scrum and look at the Scrum Board. Team members report the status for the cards they are working on. Most cards take a few days, sometimes more than a week, to get done. So it's toward the end of a Sprint that people start reporting that they are at risk of not finishing. By then, of course, the testers don't have enough time."

Based on our experience, possible root causes include the following issues:

- Not understanding the purpose of the Daily Scrum and poor facilitation of the Daily Scrum (Empiricism, Teamwork, Team Process)

- Lack of shared purpose among the Development Team and not holding each other accountable (Teamwork, Team Identity)

- Silos in knowledge and skills that prevent collaboration and getting items completed earlier in the Sprint (Teamwork, Team Identity, Team Process)

Given the answers provided, ask the following kinds of questions to refine your understanding:

- How much transparency is there to the progress of work on a daily basis?
- Why do team members work on different things?
- How does the Scrum Team adapt when it discovers that there is not enough time to finish everything?

There are many ways this example conversation could unfold, and in practice it will take longer and require more questions to find the root causes of the problem. Major pain points are often complex and have multiple root causes. Consequently, you will have to prioritize which paths you go down first. You will start to see themes or patterns develop. Look for the root causes that are foundational, meaning they will prevent progress in solving other issues essential to the effectiveness of Scrum.

Scrum Teams can use this technique in Sprint Retrospectives to help them understand why they are experiencing a particular problem (see Figure 1-1).

In Figure 1-1, a Scrum Team's three major pain points are circled, and each possible cause is shown as contributing to one or more of the pain points. Now that they have visualized the problems and root causes, the Scrum Team can make better-informed decisions about where to start to fix the most critical issues. Although there is no magic formula to address all possible root causes, an iterative and incremental approach will allow the team to discover the best options for them at this point of time. Improving incrementally is done by employing empiricism. By discussing challenges and their possible root causes, you have created transparency and enabled inspection of that transparent information.

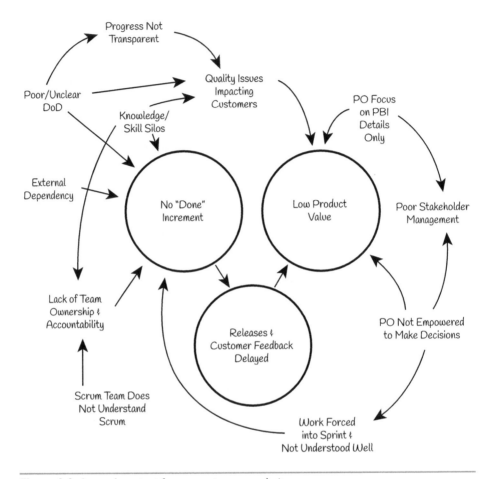

Figure 1-1 A sample output from a root cause analysis

EXPERIMENT WITH DIFFERENT APPROACHES

Complex problems don't have simple or obvious solutions. Before you make a major investment in a particular solution, make sure that you understand the problem and have a viable solution for fixing it. Regardless of the data, intuition, and experience you have, there will always be some things that you don't know.

To move forward without being paralyzed by these unknowns, you can try some experiments to see what might work or to gather more information.[8] Sounds very in alignment with navigating complexity and unpredictability, eh?

To effectively use experiments to improve, follow these steps:

1. Identify the problem you are trying to solve. You've probably got some ideas about this from your root cause analysis.
2. Create a hypothesis about some action that you think you can take to improve.
3. Decide what you will do to test this hypothesis.
4. Run the experiment.
5. Analyze the results. This includes comparing actual results against expectations, reflecting on learning, and getting feedback.
6. Refine and repeat. This may include modifying the hypothesis or the experiment.

When you design the experiment, be clear about the following points:

- What are you trying to learn?
- How will you measure success?
- How soon can you get feedback?

When you design the experiment, you also want to consider the potential return on investment (ROI) of the experiment. Ideally, the experiment should be reasonably small, so you can minimize the investment and get feedback sooner. The experiment should also provide sufficient value. The low-hanging fruit may be fast and easy to pick, but you may get less return from it. The higher-value things may take more investment, time, and energy.

---

8. Trying things out in a structured and disciplined way is the foundation for the scientific method; see https://www.britannica.com/science/scientific-method.

There is no one right answer. You have to consider your team's unique pain points and unique needs. You have to get creative about breaking down the big stuff into smaller experiments of higher value. By doing so, you can improve iteratively and incrementally.

Now you know where you are—and you know where you want to be. As you start identifying experiments to run in an effort to move closer to where you want to be, create an improvement backlog. Order these items and begin.

In the same way that Scrum uses an empirical approach to solve complex problems and deliver valuable products, you can use an empirical approach to solve complex problems and maximize the benefits of Scrum. You can do this at the Scrum Team level and at other levels of the organization beyond the Scrum Team. For an individual Scrum Team, this cycle of continuous improvement is already built into the cadence of a Sprint and the use of a Sprint Retrospective to inspect and adapt as a Scrum Team. In addition, it is up to each Scrum Team to determine the amount of time that needs to be devoted to improvement each Sprint and how to organize and validate the improvements made each Sprint.

SUCCESS OR FAILURE?

Is it possible for a success to be a failure? Is it possible for a failure to be a success?

You may have noticed that many of the Business Agility assessment questions in Appendix A deal with outcomes (e.g., value, quick delivery). Although outcomes are most important, behaviors can also be important when they help build a team's capabilities.

You cannot control all of the variables in complex work and the unpredictable environmental conditions around you. If you could, then you would plan everything out in advance, follow that plan, and obtain guaranteed results. In the messy real world, however, you may do all the "right things" and still not get the desired outcomes. This is why it is important to look at behaviors as well.

As you analyze the results of your experiments or improvement steps, consider both outcomes and behaviors, especially their trends over time. For example, consider the situation in which a Development Team uncovers major technical challenges with a new integration. The Development Team started this work on the first day of the Sprint because team members knew it would be more challenging and had previously learned the hard way that they should tackle the riskier items sooner. They swarmed. They informed the Product Owner of the situation and worked together to break the work down smaller. Ultimately, though, they didn't get to "Done."

In this example, there is a clear failure: The team does not have a "Done" Increment. Yet there is also a success: The team applied learning from their previous experience and did the best they could with what they knew at the time. They collaborated, negotiated, and adapted throughout the Sprint. The key is to find new learning to do even better next time. Perhaps the team will decide to adjust how they do Product Backlog refinement to break items down in a different way. Maybe they will identify a skill gap to address. Maybe they will decide to change their development practices or tools.

Ultimately, there are two questions to ask:

- Did we do the best we could with what we knew at the time?
- How can we do better?

SUMMARY

The seven key improvement areas we focus on—an agile mindset, empiricism, teamwork, team process, team identity, product value, and organization—provide a lens through which you can inspect your team's ability to achieve its goals and find ways to improve. By looking for underlying root causes, running experiments to try to improve, and then inspecting and adapting, you can gradually, consistently, and continuously improve your ability to achieve better results.

The seven key areas also provide a lens through which you can observe outcomes and behaviors. You can look for underlying root causes, peeling the onion. This lens creates focus and clarity so that you can reflect and take intentional action.

You improve empiricism by employing empiricism. You must create transparency about the desired outcomes of the improvements and regularly inspect and adapt your way toward maximizing the benefits of Scrum.

CALL TO ACTION

Review your notes from your self-assessment questions and ratings and consider the following points:

- What do you notice about the data?
- What trends do you see?
- What new insights did you gain from this assessment?

Using what we have discussed in this chapter for guidance, hold a collaborative discussion with your Scrum Team to take the following steps:

1. Identify the top two or three pain points.
2. For each one, identify possible root causes.
3. Choose two or three root causes to address.
4. Create an ordered list of the first improvements you want to implement. For each of these "experiments," be sure to clarify expected outcomes and how you will measure results.
5. Begin.

Creating a Strong Team Foundation

Agile success starts with a strong team. Ideally that team is cohesive, cross-functional, and self-organizing, though most teams start out as a collection of individuals who have to learn how to work with each other to achieve their shared goals. Members of new Scrum Teams, especially those who are not used to working as part of a cross-functional team, often struggle at first to produce "Done" Product Increments in every Sprint. In this chapter, we consider how teams can overcome these challenges.

Forming a Team Identity

You cannot simply put a group of people together, tell them "You are a team," and expect them to achieve great things. Forming a team means making an investment in bringing a group of people together to achieve something they could not achieve by themselves. Together, the team members form an entirely new living and breathing organism that develops an identity over time.

At a fundamental level, establishing a team's identity is shaped by answering three questions that guide a team on its journey toward performing:

- Why do we exist—what is our purpose?
- What is important to us—what values do we hold dear?
- What do we want to achieve, together?

Just as we do as individuals, every team will constantly refine and clarify its identity as its members learn and grow. A team's beliefs about its identity help it (or hinder it) on its journey toward achieving shared goals and continuously improving its effectiveness. In the context of agile product development, an agile mindset provides a helpful starting point in forming a Scrum Team's identity.[1]

What Makes a Good Team Member?

We are human, and as such we make mistakes, even though we may have good intentions. We want to do the best we can. We want to grow and learn. We are all capable of much more than we know. We thrive when we feel a sense of connection and have community. We are also wonderfully unique.

Even in a team environment, understanding and appreciating the individual is important. Although individuals need to let go of their individual status and ego to focus on team goals and outcomes, each person on the team still has his or her own needs to be met. After all, engaged and fulfilled people will be more creative and productive and probably even more enjoyable to work with.

---

1. For ideas on how to leverage the Scrum values and the Agile Manifesto values (www.agilemanifesto.org) to refine a team's identity, see https://www.scrum.org/resources/blog/maximize-scrum-scrum-values-focus-part-1-5.

Three aspects are important to consider to appreciate the unique skills and talents that team members will bring to the team and to understand how being part of that team may help those individuals grow and find fulfillment:

- *Personality.* People are wonderfully unique; they have different personalities, which show up as preferences and behaviors that tend to persist across a lifespan. Some characteristics are genetic in origin, whereas others are shaped by experiences. However, people can consciously choose to act differently than their innate preferences so as to meet the team's desired goals.[2]

  Personality differences create conflict, but these same differences create diversity that expands perspectives in ways that make teams more innovative and effective.[3] When teams are effective, team members figure out how to navigate conflict in healthy ways.

- *Emotional intelligence.* Emotional intelligence is about understanding and managing your own emotions and behaviors and being able to recognize and influence the emotions of others.[4] Emotional intelligence helps people understand when and how to express their personality traits.

  According to research by TalentSmart, emotional intelligence comprises a flexible set of skills that can be improved with practice. Although some people naturally have higher emotional intelligence than others, you can acquire and grow this skill set. Furthermore, TalentSmart has found that 90 percent of top performers are also high in emotional intelligence. On the flip side, just 20 percent of bottom performers are high in emotional intelligence.[5] This makes sense when we think about the nature of product development.

- *Intrinsic motivation.* While motivation matters for all work, self-organizing teams simply are not effective unless each team member is intrinsically motivated. As Dan Pink notes in *Drive*, knowledge workers are not

---

2. https://carleton.ca/economics/wp-content/uploads/little08.pdf

3. https://hbr.org/2013/12/how-diversity-can-drive-innovation

4. For more background on emotional intelligence, see Daniel Goleman's *Emotional Intelligence: Why It Can Matter More Than IQ* (Bantam Books, 2005).

5. Travis Bradbury and Jean Greaves, *Emotional Intelligence 2.0* (TalentSmart, 2009).

motivated by extrinsic rewards like money; instead, they are motivated by three factors:[6]

- *Autonomy.* People are in control of how they do their work.

- *Mastery.* People have the ability to become great at something, to grow and sharpen their knowledge and skills.

- *Purpose.* People feel they are working on something bigger than themselves. They see meaning in their work.

In Practice: Personality and Emotional Intelligence

A Scrum Team has built up frustration with a team member named Alex whom team members say is "negative," "antagonistic," and "flippant." The new Scrum Master has been getting these complaints from individuals for a few weeks. She has also closely observed interactions between Alex and the rest of the team and senses that Alex's personality puts him low on the agreeableness scale.[7]

Through a series of one-on-one conversations with Alex and team members, as well as leveraging opportunities presented in team discussions about their work, the Scrum Master helps create a better understanding of differences in personality and the benefits they provide. Team members begin to realize that Alex is not trying to be negative or skeptical of their ideas. His nature is simply to question things first in an attempt to understand better, to ensure that there has been sufficient exploration. They even begin to appreciate and seek his input more often. Alex also has a better understanding of how his comments can be perceived negatively by team members and even feel hurtful, and he is more mindful of how he questions and explores his colleagues' ideas.

By learning more about their own and each other's personalities, team members are better able to choose how they show up in their daily interactions. In turn, they are better able to achieve desired outcomes while feeling more ease in how they work together.

---

6. Dan Pink's book *Drive* (Riverhead Books, 2011) provides a compelling discussion of what motivates people working on complex intellectual tasks, which is summarized in the following short video: https://www.youtube.com/watch?v=u6XAPnuFjJc. For more information, see https://www.danpink.com/drive.

7. While many models for understanding personality preferences have been developed, the factor agreeableness comes from the Five Factor Model. See https://positivepsychology.com/big-five-personality-theory.

Successful teams are composed of team members who are self-aware enough to understand their own strengths, have sufficient emotional intelligence to adapt their reactions to those around them, and are intrinsically motivated to work with others to achieve things that they could not achieve on their own.[8]

WHO SHOULD BE ON A SCRUM TEAM?

In a perfect world in which everyone has all the skills that a team might need, we would say that the answer to this question is "anyone who wants to be on the Scrum Team." In reality, when you need to keep the number of people on the team small enough to manage the complexity of communication, and you need a lot of different skills to deliver a "Done" Product Increment in every Sprint, you have to make wise choices and thoughtful trade-offs about who is on the Scrum Team and who is not. Then, as a team, you must work within the constraints established by those choices.

Over time, you will need to continuously improve your skills. As a team, you do the best that you can with the skills that you have today and then work to grow skills to fill any gaps. Being on a cross-functional team means that team members are willing to do things to contribute to overall success even if they may not be the best or the fastest at doing that thing. Such teams figure out how to leverage the skills and knowledge they have as a whole, and they take action to grow when they discover gaps and bottlenecks that are slowing them down. Over time, this means that they will gradually develop more and different kinds of "deep" skills (see Figure 2-1).[9]

---

8. For more on the skills and traits that individuals can grow to become better at teamwork, see *Teamwork Is an Individual Skill* by Christopher Avery (ReadHowYouWant, 2012) and *The Ideal Team Player* by Patrick Lencioni (Jossey-Bass, 2016).

9. "T-shaped skills" is a metaphor for a person having broad problem-solving or business domain skills as well as deeper skills in an area of specialty (see https://en.wikipedia.org/wiki/T-shaped_skills). Pi and comb-shaped skills simply refer to a person having deep skills in more than one area of specialty.

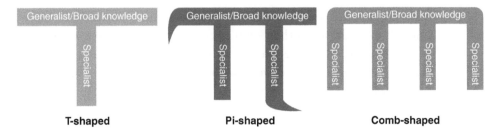

Figure 2-1 Over time, team members tend to develop deep skills in more areas.

Development Teams own their cross-functionality. Indeed, this is a key aspect of self-organization. A Development Team may choose to add someone to the team to gain more skills and knowledge. Team members may also choose to get formal training or spend time on self-directed learning so as to develop broader and deeper skills and knowledge. In addition, a Development Team may choose to work in a way that supports mentoring aimed at further growing existing team members. As the product and the team evolve, the distribution of skills and knowledge across team members will need to evolve as well.

DEVELOPMENT TEAMS NEED TO KNOW ABOUT MORE THAN JUST DEVELOPMENT

When you think about the skills required to deliver a "Done" Product Increment to customers or real users, consider the following questions:

- Is it useful for Development Team members to understand how the product is used by customers?
- Is it useful for Development Team members to understand how product changes might impact business processes or other products used by customers or in the organization?
- Is it useful for Development Team members to understand how their product may be affected by changes to other products, business processes, and policies in the organization?

Of course, the answer to all these questions is, most emphatically, yes! Business analysis skills are an important part of delivering a working

Increment of value, but this doesn't always mean that you need a Business Analyst on the Development Team; you have to move beyond the old ways of building products.

What if someone with this business context joins the Development Team? How can this person's knowledge and experience and skills contribute to the work in a Sprint? Perhaps the new member can answer questions to guide the direction of a Product Backlog item (PBI) while it is being developed. Perhaps this individual can contribute to improving quality by offering input on testing approaches and test case details and by assisting with the testing effort itself. Perhaps the member can play a role in developing online help, training materials, or business change management activities. Perhaps he or she can contribute to Product Backlog refinement. All of these contributions will help the Development Team meet its definition of "Done."

Not everyone on a Development Team has to know how to write code, and creating a valuable "Done" Increment requires much more than just writing code.

How Do Scrum Teams Form Working Agreements?

Working agreements help a group of individuals with different personalities, preferences, and experiences work together effectively by being explicit about what commitment to the team looks like. Keep in mind that working agreements are not the Scrum Master's rules to enforce. Instead, the entire Scrum Team takes on this responsibility: Team members hold each other accountable and address issues as they arise. Working agreements are not static, however, and teams should regularly revisit and update them as the team evolves.

Working agreements often address three areas:

- Tasks, or the expected activities and deliverables for the team
- Process, or how the activities will be carried out
- Norms, or the ways in which team members will interact with each other

Creating a working agreement contributes to the formation of a strong team identity. Working agreements are born out of the values and principles that the team members hold dear, and developing working agreements often makes these values and principles concrete. Such an agreement establishes a foundation on which the team can self-organize. A team is more committed to team success over individual success when all members share a common set of values and principles. It is also easier to commit to team decisions even if an individual has some concerns when that person knows those decisions are grounded in values and principles.

Asking the following questions may help you develop your team's working agreement:

- What are our standards of quality, and how will we ensure we meet them?
- How will we collaborate effectively?
- How will we share information within the team and with stakeholders?
- What are our standards for meeting attendance, promptness, and participation?
- How will we make decisions?
- How will we surface conflict or disagreements?
- How do we want it to be when we are in conflict?
- How will the Scrum values guide our interactions and our work?
- How will we grow knowledge and skills across team members?
- What does respectful behavior look like for us?
- How will we monitor our performance and progress?
- How will we hold each other accountable for our commitments?

The Development Team's definition of "Done" is also a working agreement about how team members will ensure quality and completeness of a Product Increment.

In Practice: The Team Purpose Statement

Helping a team construct its own purpose statement (see Figure 2-2) can be a useful way to bring the team together and to bring clarity and transparency to its working agreements. A purpose statement addresses the following elements:

- What: what customer needs the team is attempting to fill
- How: the methods or technologies the team will use to fill those customer needs
- Who: a description of the primary customer(s)
- Why: the reasons why it is important to fill those customer needs
- Special Sauce: what makes the team different

> We provide easy-to-use content management solutions so that our users can be more effective in doing their jobs and serving customers, trusting they are in compliance with all regulatory, legal, and security standards.

Figure 2-2 A sample team purpose statement.

WHAT DOES SELF-ORGANIZATION LOOK LIKE?

A self-organizing Scrum Team is able to determine how it does its work. In practice, this can manifest itself in a variety of ways:

- Scrum Teams take ownership of their processes. They don't blame the process. They change things that aren't working well and challenge the organizational processes that are impeding them.
- Scrum Teams determine a Sprint Goal together. Development Teams decide how much work they can forecast in a Sprint together. Development Teams decide how they will do the work together.
- Development Team members don't wait until the Daily Scrum to bring up challenges or impediments.

- Development Team members decide how and when to swarm problems that jeopardize the Sprint Goal.
- Development Team members update their Sprint Backlog to reflect current progress and new learning.
- Scrum Teams determine how they will improve as a team and take ownership of implementing these actionable commitments in every Sprint.
- Scrum Team members address and resolve their own disagreements and conflicts.
- Scrum Teams make consensus-based decisions in a timely manner. They determine if they need to consult outside expertise.

Effective self-organization requires three things: shared goals, clear accountabilities, and boundaries (see Figure 2-3). If any of these weaken, the team may lose the ability to self-organize and become less effective.

Figure 2-3 Effective self-organization requires all three legs to stay balanced.

SHARED GOALS

All great teams need a goal—the more audacious, the better. They need something toward which they can strive and stretch, and an achievement against which they can measure themselves. Without shared goals, it is easy for team members to follow divergent paths and for a team to lose purpose and cohesion.

Shared goals usually start with the goals for the product, expressed in terms of a clearly articulated business strategy, a well-defined product vision, a clear understanding of customer value, and a clear way to measure it. All of these aspects provide guidance that helps teams see where they are headed and what is important.

The Sprint Goal is also important and provides an overarching purpose or objective for the Scrum Team while conducting the Sprint. It provides focus as the team uncovers new information and encounters challenges while building the Increment during the Sprint. You can look at Sprint Goals as the waypoints that make up the path to meeting bigger, longer-term release or business goals.

Getting even more granular, every day the Daily Scrum is focused on the work that the Development Team will undertake in the next 24 hours to progress toward the Sprint Goal.

CLEAR ACCOUNTABILITY

Scrum provides clear accountabilities for each role. The organization must respect these accountabilities. This means ensuring Scrum Team members are given the authority to fulfill their roles. Team members also need the knowledge and skills to fulfill their accountabilities. This may require an investment in knowledge transfer and training. It may also mean giving people access to information to help guide decisions.

Of course, Scrum Team members need sufficient time to fulfill their roles. When team members have multiple responsibilities beyond their Scrum role, it is important to assess the impact this may have. Which role takes priority? Do individuals have sufficient time to fulfill their Scrum role? How about their other roles? What happens when the individual has to make a difficult choice to let something drop to fulfill the Scrum role, or vice versa?

Furthermore, if a misalignment occurs between how individual performance is assessed and what individual members are accountable for, this can create a dilemma for team members to navigate. Should they do what is in their own best interest for the purposes of having a "good performance review"? Or should they do what's best to fulfill their Scrum role?

What it takes to fulfill the Product Owner role, the Development Team role, and the Scrum Master role will change over time as the product, the business, and the Scrum Team evolve. To ensure that these needs can be addressed, it is important for Scrum Teams to continue assessing what is needed now and in the near future.

BOUNDARIES

The Scrum Framework, including its 11 elements and the rules that bind them together, provides boundaries that make it "safe" for the Scrum Team to self-organize. By "safe," we mean that the risk of failure is reduced and the cost of failure is limited.

Time-boxes in Scrum are an example of boundaries that provide focus, create a sense of urgency, reduce waste, and limit risk. Consider how the use of time-boxes is providing these benefits to the team or where their benefits may be lacking.

A "Done" Increment is required at least by the end of a Sprint, and a definition of "Done" provides a clear boundary of what quality and completeness means to a Development Team. Note that an organization may have a minimum baseline definition of "Done"—this is an example of the organization setting the minimal boundary that a Development Team can then build upon.

There may be a need to establish and clarify boundaries beyond the Scrum Framework. These boundaries may relate to technology decisions, team development, or many other categories. Ask these kinds of questions to clarify boundaries:

• What decisions is the Scrum Team empowered to make?
• Who does the team need to consult for certain types of decisions?
• Who does the team need to inform when it makes certain types of decisions?

For example, a Scrum Team may need to consult with an Enterprise Architecture group when team members want to bring a new technology into their product platform. They may simply need to inform an Enterprise Architecture group when they are making changes that grow the size of their product platform.

Another example is the decisions that a Scrum Team can make regarding team development. A Scrum Team is autonomous in how its members work together to build the Increment, teaching and mentoring each other to grow skills, but the team may have to consult a manager when it wants to invest more than a specific dollar amount for training and other learning resources.

Leadership and Self-Organization

Leadership is essential for creating the conditions for effective self-organization. In *Turn the Ship Around!*, David Marquet describes the relationships among the three factors of control (i.e., giving more control), competence, and clarity as a means to create a space of intent-based leadership.

The leader's job is to support Development Teams in their efforts to increase their overall competence. The leader can help teams build competence and clarity and then give them more control. Alternatively, the leader can give more control first and then fill in the competence and clarity. The way to rapidly change and improve is to give more control first, which requires that leaders trust their teams. It is easier for them to do this when they have the boundary of a Sprint to create focus and minimize the impacts of failure.

People develop competence and clarity fastest when they learn by doing the work—that is the essence of empiricism! Even when they come up short of their goals, they learn new things that help them move closer to the goal the next time they try. Some agilists refer to this approach as "failing fast" but, in truth, the only real failure is failure to learn from experiments.

HOW DO SCRUM TEAMS COLLABORATE?

A self-organizing, cross-functional team needs to learn how to collaborate. To do that, team members need to invest in building "collaborative assets." Five assets help teams reap the benefits of effective collaboration:[10]

- Trust
- Productive conflict
- Commitment
- Accountability
- Shared goals and outcomes

These assets, as depicted in Figure 2-4, build upon one another. If you don't have trust, it will be impossible to have the other four assets. If you don't have productive conflict, it will be impossible to have commitment, accountability, and shared goals. And so on for each asset.

Figure 2-4 These assets form building blocks for effective team collaboration.

Trust, in this context, means willingness to be vulnerable with one's fellow team members, such as willingness to admit a mistake or ask for help. When team members trust each other, they are open to productive conflict: They are

---

10. If you have read Patrick Lencioni's leadership fable *The Five Dysfunctions of a Team* (*Jossey-Bass, 2002*), these assets may seem familiar. In his highly acclaimed book, Lencioni presents five dysfunctions. Here we focus on the opposite of these dysfunctions—that is, the assets of collaborative teams.

willing to challenge each other, to challenge assumptions, and to be open to and share what they think may be wild and crazy ideas.[11]

In Practice: Building Trust

Trust is a willingness to be vulnerable, a willingness to make something important to you be vulnerable to the actions of others. People who work in an atmosphere of trust can collaborate productively, enabling things to get done faster and at a lower cost. Conversely, when trust is absent, business slows down and costs rise as people spend more time trying to protect themselves against those whom they cannot trust.[12]

There is no one sure way to build trust, and there are countless ways to destroy it. We see trust as an ongoing journey that is more about consistency in how you show up in your relationships and interactions. This journey is never complete, and you can easily move backward. Here are some techniques that we use to build trust:[13]

- *Go first.* You may need to be the one to give trust first before you have it returned. Be vulnerable to show others it is okay to be vulnerable. Ask for help. Admit your mistakes.

- *Be willing to say no.* When you overcommit, you put yourself at risk for not following through and negatively impacting others. You can be perceived as unreliable.

- *Assume positive intent.* Do your best to always assume positive intent about another person's actions or words. While it may be appropriate to address a situation when someone's actions or words have had negative outcomes, have that conversation assuming the person had good intentions. This helps you address the conflict, resolve issues, and come to a better understanding of each other while showing you trust the other person.

- *Avoid gossiping.* Talking about people is often perceived as an easy way to make conversation and bond with others. However, the unintended consequence is that it makes you appear to be untrustworthy. If you talk about someone and share something that person told you in confidence with me, how do I know that you wouldn't do the same with something I told you in confidence?

---

11. For more on this topic, see https://www.agilesocks.com/build-trust-enable-agility/.
12. The *Speed of Trust* by Stephen M. R. Covey (Free Press, 2008).
13. For a deeper insight into building trust, see https://brenebrown.com/videos/anatomy-trust-video/.

- *Match your words to your actions.* Make sure that you live up to what you profess to believe is important. If you tell your team that sustainable pace is important, yet you work long hours and answer emails on the weekends, there is a misalignment between your stated beliefs and your actions.

- *Be open and honest with people.* Creating an environment in which people can be open and honest about their feelings, their concerns, and their desires is essential for trust. You may have to go first, leading by example. When creating working agreements, ask team members what agreements they need to be open and honest with each other.

- *When you make mistakes, share the learning.* Rather than focusing on blaming (or worse, shaming), help everyone recognize that every mistake is a learning opportunity. Encourage team members to share their own learning opportunities with the team. You may have to go first, leading by example. Refer to your own mistakes when teaching moments arise.

- *Get to know each other as people.* Encourage team members to see each other as people with rich experiences and full lives beyond the office. Create situations that help people bond over their personal stories. You may sensitively ask about family, friends, hobbies, or interests. Consider starting by sharing personal information about yourself first.

Conflict, in this context, means using conflict in productive ways to generate new ideas and explore different solutions. Effective teams use the diverse perspectives of their members to constructively challenge and improve solutions. Passionate arguments, when conducted with mutual respect and while seeking the best possible outcome, are sometimes the catalyst that enables breakthrough solutions. Productive conflict involves questioning the status quo, challenging assumptions, and overcoming limiting beliefs.

In Practice: Navigating the Conflict Spectrum

Once team members trust one another, they can exploit the power of productive conflict. Sometimes the team may even want to seek out conflict to deal with complex issues, whereas at other times they will want to defuse conflict.

So how does a team know if conflict is productive? When conflict exists because team members have different viewpoints but still share a common commitment to achieving the best outcomes for their customers, stakeholders, and organization. If conflict makes you a little uncomfortable, keep in mind that positive conflict always emerges from a desire to change for the better.

It helps to understand your own natural response to conflict, which is an element of your personality. It's not right or wrong; it's simply a preference. You may choose to override that initial preference, if you are aware of it.[14]

Conflict tends to escalate in a graduated way. It may start with simple differences in perspectives and ideas. Perhaps personal factors and environmental factors might then contribute to conflict progressing in ways that are driven by a need to protect oneself, to be validated, or to uphold deeply ingrained belief systems. Also, people may turn to techniques such as forming coalitions, undermining, or even threatening. What is important is to recognize the level of conflict and respond in ways that move people toward a shared commitment to seek the best possible outcomes.

Being able to engage in and resolve conflict productively is important for self-organizing teams. Some teams may need help in the form of learning how to engage in productive conflict. Other teams may need help with facilitating the de-escalation of unhealthy conflict. And in some cases (e.g., harassment, risk of physical or emotional harm), immediate action may be needed to intervene, separate, and take appropriate steps.[15]

---

14. The Thomas–Kilman Instrument (TKI) is one tool for understanding conflict response modes.
15. We encourage you to look for additional resources to understand models for conflict. We will offer two to explore here, but keep in mind that the best model is one that helps you and your team engage in productive conflict. While Speed Leas applied his Levels of Conflict model in religious organizations, it has been embraced in the agile community and written about here: https://dzone.com/articles/agile-managing-conflict. Another model to consider is Friedrich Glasl's nine-stage model of conflict escalation: https://www.mediate.com/articles/jordan.cfm.

Commitment, in this context, means that once the team resolves conflicts and reaches consensus, team members are committed to the decision because they perceive that their ideas and perspectives are respected by their fellow team members. We often use the phrase "disagree and commit" to reflect that team members may still hold to their own opinions, but they commit to their fellow team members to respect the team's decision.

In Practice: Facilitating Consensus

The consensus techniques described here are ways to gather quick and transparent data about where a team stands on a decision. Here are a few examples of when these techniques could be used:

- To determine the Sprint events schedule.
- To confirm the Development Team's agreement on the Sprint Goal and the Sprint Backlog.
- During collaboration sessions for design or architecture approaches.
- In Product Backlog refinement sessions to determine how to break down features/functions into smaller PBIs and/or how and when to run experiments for feedback and learning.

The assumption when you use these techniques is that sufficient discussion has already happened to ensure everyone's ideas have been explored for shared understanding, and everyone has been heard.

Fist of Five is a consensus technique that allows groups of people to quickly understand where they agree or disagree. People indicate their level of support by holding up one hand and indicating a number. It may take a few rounds of discussion and check-in to reach a consensus-based decision. You can use time-boxes to help keep the discussions focused and avoid getting into analysis paralysis.[16]

---

16. For more information, see Jean Tabaka's book *Collaboration Explained: Facilitation Skills for Software Project Leaders* (Addison-Wesley Professional, 2006).

> **Roman Voting** is derived from how the Romans indicated their will in the gladi-atorial arena. With this technique, people indicate their level of support with a thumbs-up, thumbs-sideways, or thumbs-down gesture:
>
> - Thumbs-up means *I support this.*
> - Thumbs-sideways means *I will go along with the will of the group.*
> - Thumbs-down means *I do not support this and wish to address the group.*
>
> If all thumbs are down or all thumbs are up, you have quite clear consensus. In case of a mixed vote, be sure to allow people with thumbs-down to speak. Be cautious of decisions where all thumbs are sideways because the group may have some artificial harmony or unhealthy conflict that needs to be explored at a deeper level.[17]

Accountability, in this context, means that team members hold each other accountable for the commitments they have made. It takes courage to challenge a fellow team member for not upholding commitments. Because accountability is built on trust, along with the knowledge that everyone shares the same goals, the inherent conflict in these conversations is defused and channeled toward productive discussions about how to move forward.

Team members holding each other accountable is more effective than management holding teams accountable. This is also why commitment is the building block that leads to holding each other accountable. Team members will feel more accountable for their *own* commitments than for commitments others make on their behalf.

When team members are willing to hold each other accountable, they enable the team to set and meet higher standards. This could show up as higher quality, better solutions, greater learning, and more innovation.

When there is accountability within a team, it is then possible to focus on shared goals and outcomes.

---

17. https://www.mountaingoatsoftware.com/blog/four-quick-ways-to-gain-or-assess-team-consensus

HOW DO TEAMS PROGRESS?

Teamwork is essential, but it doesn't happen automatically, and it doesn't usually happen quickly. Most teams go through a series of stages as they come together and build the assets they need for effective collaboration. Bruce Tuckman's model of group development is one way to view the changes that a team goes through as members learn to work together (see Figure 2-5). Some teams never progress beyond the lower levels, and teams can fall back to earlier stages when setbacks occur, new members join, or key members leave.

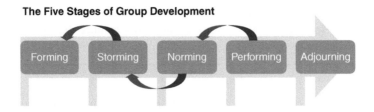

Figure 2-5 Tuckman's model of group development[18]

When teams are *forming*, they are trying to understand each other. They may be reserved in their interactions. They avoid conflict while they work to establish boundaries.

As differences begin to surface (remember the discussion about personalities) and team members become more dependent on each other, conflicts begin to arise. Tuckman calls this stage *storming*.

As teams begin to channel their conflict more productively and gain a better understanding of how they can work more effectively together, they are said to be *norming*. Members begin to focus on team goals and set standards for quality and effectiveness. They are committed to the team and take pride in being part of the team and the work they produce as a whole.

---

18. See https://project-management.com/the-five-stages-of-project-team-development for more background on Tuckman's model and its application to team development. While Tuckman's model appears to show that teams progress in a linear fashion, the reality is much more complex. Nevertheless, the model provides a perspective on how teams evolve.

As the team evolves together, members begin to operate more smoothly and autonomously. They are now *performing*. You will see passionate debate among team members because they are committed and dedicated to creating the best outcomes, keeping high standards, and continuously improving themselves. While they cannot predict the future, they exude a confidence that as a team they can meet any challenge.

Adjourning occurs when a team disbands. This termination can be quite stressful, especially when it happens suddenly and is unplanned. Even the best teams can find this stage disorienting and demotivating.

In reality, teams move between these stages in response to external events. A *performing* team can run into new challenges that require members to expand their skills and knowledge, and the resulting uncertainty and conflict may pull them back to *norming*, or even *forming*, if they have to add new team members.

In Practice: Dealing with Setbacks

Here is a situation that we run into quite often: A team that has been *performing* decided in its last Sprint Retrospective to improve the test automation, forcing team members to learn new techniques and technologies. Pushed out of their comfort zone, they struggle to learn new skills while also trying to complete other work during the Sprint. Conflicts and frustration emerge, and their forecasted productivity drops.

The next Sprint Review does not go well. Not only did the team members not achieve all that they had forecast, but they also did not make much progress on automating tests. In their Sprint Retrospective, they recognize that they did not anticipate the degree to which their team's working relationships would be affected, or the effort that automation would require. Team members agree to be more mindful of these changes as they plan the next Sprint.

Stronger teams with supportive leadership and a learning culture will recover more quickly from such backtracking, whereas teams in organizations that seek to lay blame for setbacks may never recover.[19]

---

19. For more on learning cultures, see Peter M. Senge, *The Fifth Discipline: The Art & Practice of Learning Organization* (New York: Doubleday/Currency, 1990).

In Practice: How Stable Does a Team's Composition Need to Be?

A stable team is one whose team members don't split their time too much with other teams and whose team composition doesn't change too much over time. Members of a stable team can form better working relationships because they spend more time together, which allows time for the members to develop trust in each other. These teams also tend to be more familiar with the product and the business domain because they spend more time working on a single product.

Some organizations find it difficult to maintain stable teams because their products don't need to change quickly, so they do not need a dedicated team. Furthermore, team members may want to work on different products, learn new technologies and business domains, and work with different people.

Even when team members could work on one team, the team may need to vary the skills on the team over time, so it may need to move people on and off the team. Or perhaps team members may be shared with other teams when they all need the same scarce skills.

Virginia Satir created a five-stage change model that describes the effects that each stage has on feelings, thinking, performance, and physiology.[20] As depicted in Figure 2-6, at the point of change, the team enters *resistance* where it experiences a decline in performance. This change interrupts stability and familiarity, and some individuals may be in denial, avoidance, or even blocking mode. *Chaos* is the period of erratic performance that occurs while the team members search for a way to deal with and incorporate the change in their world. When they find this transforming idea, they enter *integration*. During this time, performance trends upward as the team integrates this new change and even sees how it can be beneficial. Ultimately, team members find a *new status quo* in which they have fully assimilated the change.

When we implement planned change, such as adding a team member, we are hoping that the new status quo will be greater than the old status quo. But, of course, there is no guarantee that we will achieve this improvement.

---

20. https://stevenmsmith.com/ar-satir-change-model/

So what's the answer? The goal is "stable enough." The goal is for the Scrum Team to find a dynamic stability—that the team can recover quickly from a change, whether planned or unplanned. When you are implementing a planned change such as adding or removing team members to an existing team and when you are forming new teams, involve team members in the decision-making process. When possible, let them own the decision. If team members have a say, it is more likely that the inevitable drop in performance will be less severe and last for a shorter time, and ultimately the team may experience higher performance from the change.

Team stability should be something you inspect and adapt to frequently. Observe behaviors and outcomes. Get input from team members. Consider how the amount of change in your team composition could be contributing to less desirable behaviors and outcomes.

Some general advice is to move work to the teams, rather than teams to the work. Amazing teams can learn new things, but growing amazing teams takes time and usually presents the greater challenge. When a team has found that magic, take advantage of it as long as it makes sense.

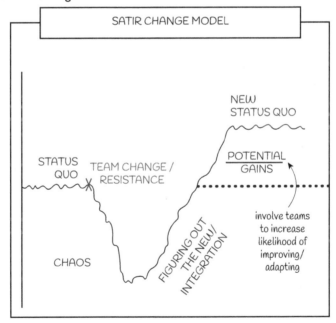

Figure 2-6 Introducing change to a team causes instability and a drop in performance.

CHARACTERISTICS OF PRODUCTIVE AND ADAPTABLE TEAMS

When Scrum Teams reach the level of performing, we expect them to be productive and adaptable, "striving to be the best they can be. It is a continuous journey toward something better."[21] When they focus on team goals rather than individual accomplishments, teams are able to create more valuable outcomes. A productive and adaptable team succeeds or fails as a team.

At the *performing* stage, Scrum Teams tend to focus on the following aspects:

- Improving the quality and completeness of a "Done" Increment
- Improving the value they deliver to customers
- Removing impediments
- Growing team skills and knowledge
- Improving their way of working through Sprint Retrospective actionable improvements

Considering the "Done" Product Increment as a shared goal, if a Scrum Team fails to deliver a releasable Increment, it has produced nothing of value and has not demonstrated business agility. It does not matter what the individuals accomplished during the Sprint—as a team they have failed to deliver a valuable outcome.

To prevent this from happening, team members adapt what they are doing and how they are doing it when challenges arise so that they can achieve the most valuable outcome in alignment with their shared goals. Productive and adaptable teams have the following characteristics:

- Are confident that, as a team, they can solve any problem
- Are committed to team success over individual success, considering both short-term and long-term impacts

---

21. See Lyssa Adkins' *Coaching Agile Teams: A Companion for ScrumMasters, Agile Coaches, and Project Managers in Transition* (Addison-Wesley Professional, 2010), page 21.

- Are driven by results and take responsibility for their results, seeking better outcomes
- Are hyper-transparent
- Make value-driven, consensus-based decisions
- Actively seek productive conflict
- Are willing to push themselves beyond their comfort zone
- Always look to improve their effectiveness and productivity
- Are able to adapt fluidly to unexpected change
- Take responsibility for their process, tools, and interactions—if something isn't working, team members take ownership of changing their experience

Which of these characteristics do you recognize in teams you work with now or that you have worked with in the past? How did it feel to be part of these teams?

SUMMARY

Strong, resilient, cross-functional, and self-organizing teams provide the essential foundation for agile success. Shared values and goals bind the team together and provide team members with principles they can all align to and use to guide decision-making. While all teams will develop at their own pace, creating an environment to enable and grow self-organization, cross-functionality, and effective collaboration is essential if teams are to become high performing and to realize the benefits of Scrum.

Teams are not static, however. As their composition and goals change, they need to revisit and adapt their values and goals. As they do, they will reinforce some aspects of their identity, refine others, and develop in new ways.

CALL TO ACTION

Consider these questions with your team:

- How clear is your team's purpose, and is it understood and embraced by every team member?
- How do the Scrum values guide your team's decisions and ways of working?
- How do the values and principles of the Agile Manifesto show up in daily interactions?
- What activities can you do to help team members understand their own and their teammates' personalities better?
- Which challenges or limitations with self-organization are holding back your team?
- What assets does you team want to grow to improve collaboration?
- How much business process, product value, and user knowledge makes sense to have in your Development Team for your product today?
- What needs to change to capitalize on the benefits of dynamic stability?
- What challenges are hurting the most right now? Identify one or two experiments to help create a stronger team foundation. For each experiment, be sure to identify the desired impacts and how you will measure them.

Delivering "Done" Product Increments

At the heart of Scrum is the concept of "Done." Scrum is a framework to enable business agility, and without "Done" Product Increments, business agility cannot exist: There is no such thing as "sort-of Done" or "almost Done." Getting to "Done" requires Scrum Teams to embrace teamwork, empiricism, and an agile mindset and to mature their team process to deliver a product that enables the team to evaluate the Sprint Goal in an empirical manner.

Once they are past the *forming* stage, new Scrum Teams often continue to struggle to produce a "Done" Product Increment every Sprint. When we teach the Professional Scrum Master (PSM) course,[1] one of the most common questions we get is: "I understand why 'Done' matters, but how do we get there if we cannot do it today?"

As the team's identity grows and creates a stronger foundation, team members will simultaneously be working on clarifying and refining their process. The Scrum Framework intentionally leaves it up to the Scrum Team to determine their own process. Remember there are no "best practices" with Scrum—that is, the best practice or tool is the one that works for your product and your team in the current moment. Moreover, the team process must evolve over time to fit changing needs and new challenges.

---

1. https://www.scrum.org/courses/professional-scrum-master-training

This dynamic quality explains why it is essential for Scrum Teams to be grounded in the elements of teamwork, empiricism, and an agile mindset so that they can deliver "Done" Product Increments. Better collaboration and more effective self-organization will point the way to higher quality and faster delivery. Greater transparency relative to the workflow, progress, and quality will enable new insights and better adaptations that improve how quickly and effectively releasable Increments are produced. Clearly, the Scrum values of focus and commitment play an important role in the team getting to "Done."[2]

Throughout this chapter, we will highlight "good practices" to consider. Keep in mind, though, that the key point is understanding what the practice is aiming to do. Is it creating more transparency into progress or quality? Is it enabling productive conflict and greater commitment to team decisions? Is it establishing boundaries to create more focus and reduce risk? Look for the root causes of your challenges, and choose practices—either those presented in this chapter or those found beyond the boundaries of this book—that will help you reliably and consistently deliver "Done" Product Increments.

Although the Development Team is accountable for producing "Done" Increments, the Product Owner and Scrum Master also contribute to the team's success; there is an inherent tension between the role accountabilities that complements collaboration.[3] For that reason, this chapter is for everyone on a Scrum Team and the leaders who support and enable them.

What Is a Definition of "Done"?

The definition of "Done" (DoD) describes the Development Team's shared understanding of the work needed to create a usable, releasable Increment. This definition—often described with conventions, standards, and guidelines—needs to meet (or exceed) any existing organizational definition.

---

2. For more details on how the Scrum values help guide Scrum Teams in effective use of Scrum, read this blog post: https://guntherverheyen.com/2013/05/03/theres-value-in-the-scrum-values/.

3. For greater understanding of the accountabilities of the Scrum roles and how they work collaboratively, read this blog post: https://www.scrum.org/resources/blog/accountability-quality-agile.

The DoD needs to be achievable and appropriate for the product and the team. When the Increment meets the DoD, it is the Product Owner's choice as to whether it is released (or not). The Increment may be released many times in a Sprint (e.g., in a continuous delivery or DevOps model) or only after multiple Sprints.

The DoD must ensure that all the work applied to the Increment is integrated with prior Increments. When multiple teams are working on a product, the combined work of all the teams needs to create a "Done" Increment. The individual team definitions may vary, but they must share a baseline minimum of quality and completeness, which of course requires integration to create a releasable product.

If this concept is so important, why doesn't Scrum tell you what should be part of the DoD? Put simply, the DoD depends so much on context that creating a universal DoD would be impossible. That is, the DoD is very different for teams working on a mobile game, a medical device, an aircraft flight control system, and an international banking system. The usage of the product, business impacts, safety, and the impact of issues on the users will all influence how "Done" is defined.

BENEFITS OF A DEFINITION OF "DONE"

Having a solid DoD, and creating an Increment that meets it, has the following benefits:

- *Transparency of process.* A "Done" Increment provides the ultimate transparency into progress and value delivery. When a team does not deliver a "Done" Product Increment in a Sprint, it is a sign that the team lacks important knowledge or capabilities. This failure represents an opportunity for the Scrum Team to examine and improve their processes, their tools, and how they work together.
- *Transparency of the Increment.* When there is clarity around "Done," no one in the Scrum Team or the stakeholders should be surprised about the quality and completeness of what is being shown in the Sprint Review.

When the Increment meets the DoD, the Product Owner can release the product to customers and realize the value from that product (ROI). Assumptions about value and how the product will be received in the market can be validated.

• *Transparency about where we are.* When there is clarity around "Done," the Product Owner can better communicate with stakeholders about completed work. This allows the Product Owner to update forecasts indicating when incremental product delivery goals are likely to be achieved.

• *Transparency about where we are going.* When Product Backlog items are completed to the agreed DoD, their size and complexity can be used to forecast future work of similar size and complexity.

• *Transparency about planning a Sprint.* By gaining a clear appreciation of what is required to complete a piece of work—to get the work "Done"— the Development Team will have a better idea of what it can deliver in a Sprint.

How to Create a Definition of "Done"

While the Development Team owns the DoD, the Product Owner can participate in the creation of the DoD to better understand what it takes to create a releasable Increment of high quality. The Product Owner may also help define quality standards for the product, such as the number of concurrent users that the system needs to support or the maximum acceptable transaction duration.

The following questions are useful to stimulate a collaborative discussion about the DoD:

• What do we need to do to assist the people who will maintain the product (e.g., readable code, variable naming conventions)?

• How will we minimize technical debt (e.g., refactoring)?

• How will we test the product (e.g., unit testing, functional testing, regression testing)?

• What testing will be automated?

• What defects must be resolved (e.g., severity, type)?

- How will we meet performance and scalability requirements (e.g., transaction processing time, concurrent users)?
- Which development standards will guide us toward technical excellence?
- How will we verify conformance to our team's development standards (e.g., peer reviews)?
- How will we validate and ensure data quality?
- How will we ensure that our product is secure?
- How will we ensure that our product meets regulatory, legal, or other compliance standards?
- What do we need to do to meet branding requirements?
- What do we need to do to ensure that our product is usable by people with disabilities (e.g., American with Disabilities Act [ADA] accessibility standards)?
- What documentation is needed to release to production (e.g., online help, updates to asset management system)?

In Practice: Using "Now, Next, Future" to Create and Improve the DoD

This technique can help a team collaboratively create an initial DoD and improve it over time. It can also help teams struggling with a not-so-great DoD focus on what is most important right now and take intentional action to move forward.

1. The Development Team is invited to brainstorm everything it would want to be part of the DoD for the highest-quality and most complete Increment. Team members assume they can do anything at all—zero constraints.

2. Team members collaboratively identify the items they are capable of doing now and move them into the center of a set of nested rectangles, as shown in Figure 3-1.

3. Team members determine what would be the next improvements they want to make; they move these items into the rectangle labeled "Next."

4. Team members determine the desired future improvements, which are likely to take a significant amount of time or money to implement, and move these into the rectangle labeled "Future."

By the end of this exercise, a team should have an updated DoD, as well as the start of an ordered list of improvements to tackle in the next few Sprints. The items may need to be broken down more granularly or reworded for more clarity, so the team may choose to do this activity after the session.[4]

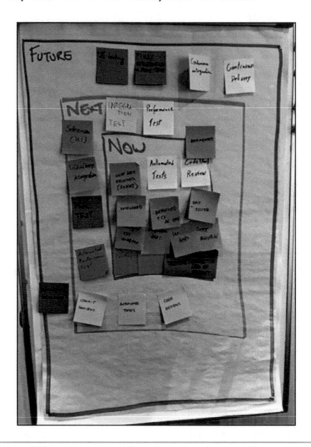

Figure 3-1 Using "Now, Next, Future" can help Development Teams define their DoD. (Photo by Simon Reindl.)

4. For more information and examples of using Now, Next, Future to improve a DoD, see https://www.scrum.org/resources/blog/improving-your-definition-done

USING SPRINT GOALS TO GET TO "DONE"

The Scrum Team commits to the Sprint Goal as the shared purpose for conducting the Sprint. When you consider the success of a Sprint, first ask, "Do we have a 'Done' Increment?"; then ask, "Did we meet the Sprint Goal?"

A good Sprint Goal has three characteristics: focus, flexibility, and purpose.

- Does it provide enough *focus* so that we can have a working Product Increment that provides value by the end of the Sprint?
- Does it provide enough *flexibility* so that we can adapt our plan (i.e., Sprint Backlog) as we uncover new learning and complexity?
- Does it provide a sense of *purpose* so that we can see the value and meaning in our work? Does it get the stakeholders excited or at least interested in attending the Sprint Review?

CREATING GOOD SPRINT GOALS

There is no perfect formula for creating a good Sprint Goal. Every Sprint Goal is very context-dependent, and Scrum Teams must experiment to find what works for them and adapt as their context changes (see Figure 3-2).[5]

Sprint Goal	Context
Improve report's load time to under 2 seconds	Team working on database-driven reports, needed to address architectural issues to address performance.
At the end of the Sprint we will show the site landing page using production-like infrastructure	Team working on a new product needed to prove the infrastructure model and the deployment process.
Expand the payment options to include more payment options	The product supported one card type provider, and needed to include other cards, PayPal, Amazon Pay, and other options. There was a lot of uncertainty, so the goal would be met if they could bring one further option.

Figure 3-2 Sample Sprint Goals.

---

5. For more information about creating good Sprint Goals, see https://www.agilesocks.com/creating-good-sprint-goals/.

The following tips will help you improve your Sprint Goals:

- *Avoid compound Sprint Goals.* Compound Sprint Goals, such as "Build X and Y and Z," split the Scrum Team's focus and do not allow flexibility. Sometimes compound Sprint Goals occur when teams are working on multiple unrelated initiatives or when they are trying to take on too much work in a Sprint. Compound Sprint Goals leave little room for the work to emerge as the Scrum Team learns.

- *Don't try to micromanage with Sprint Goals.* You do not need to include every Product Backlog item (PBI) in your Sprint Goal. In fact, a Sprint Goal that says "complete all of the PBIs" is the equivalent of not having a Sprint Goal at all. If you want self-organizing, empowered teams to be effective, you must believe that people are committed to doing their best. If the Scrum Team meets the Sprint Goal before the end of the Sprint, team members will figure out what else they can do to contribute in meaningful ways.

- *Make the Sprint Goal measurable.* When you get to the end of a Sprint, the entire team should be in agreement on whether the Sprint Goal has been achieved. To ensure the Sprint Goal is clear, ask, "How will we know if we have achieved the Sprint Goal?" during Sprint Planning, and consider if it is possible to have an objective measure.

- *Ensure team consensus on the Sprint Goal.* During Sprint Planning, use a consensus technique to confirm everyone's understanding and commitment to achieving the Sprint Goal.

- *Create Sprint Goals that achieve business impact.* People want to do meaningful work that has an impact. To ensure this, try the following:
  - *Make it business or user focused.* What will a user be able to do when you implement this feature? What will a business area be able to achieve with this enhancement?
  - *Make it focused on testing business assumptions and getting feedback.* It is difficult to know what users actually need or are willing to do (because even users don't know). A Product Owner needs early feedback to test assumptions regarding value.

- *Make it focused on reducing risk.* Proving out the use of a new technology or perhaps a new architecture is an important part of reducing risk. If you learn that a technology will not meet your needs for performance, security, or scalability, you can change direction. The earlier you change direction, the cheaper the cost of the change will be.

USING THE SPRINT GOAL FOR AN EFFECTIVE DAILY SCRUM

The Daily Scrum is intended to allow the Development Team to inspect their progress toward the Sprint Goal, adapt their plan based on new learnings so as to meet the Sprint Goal, and identify any impediments to achieving the Sprint Goal. The Daily Scrum offers an opportunity for the Development Team to recommit to each other and their shared accountability.

An effective Daily Scrum has the following characteristics:

- *Promotes self-organization and collaboration.* The Development Team facilitates the Daily Scrum, and they update their own Sprint Backlog. If everyone is focused on their commitment to the Sprint Goal and can see the progress being made toward it, there are more opportunities to contribute and collaborate.
- *Creates focus and reduces waste.* The Daily Scrum should feel like a quick collaborative planning session. A clear Sprint Goal helps everyone stay focused on the purpose of the Daily Scrum and keep it within the 15-minute time-box.
- *Promotes transparency and a shared understanding of progress of valuable outcomes.* A Daily Scrum is not simply an update on the status of tasks that each individual is working on.[6] By focusing on having a "Done" Increment that achieves the Sprint Goal, the Development Team is reminded of their purpose and commitment. Team members can assess progress in the context of the entire Sprint. If new work has been identified that endangers the Sprint Goal, they can discuss and adapt the plan. If issues are slowing progress, they can spot them early and adapt the plan.

---

6. The Daily Scrum is not a status meeting; for more on this point, see https://www.scrum.org/resources/daily-scrum-not-status-meeting.

By the end of the Daily Scrum, every Development Team member should understand progress toward the Sprint Goal, the current plan for achieving it, and the likelihood of achieving it. In addition, team members should know what they plan to accomplish in the next 24 hours and how they will work together to accomplish it. Again, using a consensus technique at the end of a Daily Scrum could be helpful to ensure everyone's voice is heard and everyone is on the same page.

GETTING PBIs TO "DONE" EARLIER IN THE SPRINT

Here are some techniques that can help you get a PBI to "Done" sooner:

- *Apply the DoD to every PBI.* Instead of waiting until the end of a Sprint to look at the DoD and perform the activities, apply the DoD to every PBI as it is worked on—and get it truly "Done" before moving on to something new. This approach has a notable side benefit: It might enable you to actually release the Product Increment before the end of the Sprint.

- *Break PBIs down to smaller items.* Smaller PBIs will likely have less complexity and unknowns, as well as less effort.

- *Try a one-day Sprint.* When a Scrum Team is struggling to break the work down into smaller increments and to collaborate on the same piece of work, a one-day Sprint can force them to challenge their assumptions. This kind of Sprint is not likely something that you'll want to do all the time, but it can be an illuminating team improvement activity that helps break down limiting beliefs and encourages creative approaches to delivering value.

  To get the team started, you can offer this challenge: "Is there any small piece of value that we can deliver to users in a day?" By shrinking the time-box, you create focus and urgency, forcing team members to try new things. They will worry less about their specializations and expertise and instead think more about contributing to the team results. There is little risk to trying a one-day Sprint: If it doesn't work, only a day has been lost.

But the potential benefit can be substantial; the insights that emerge are often quite powerful and lead to many actionable commitments for the next "regular-length" Sprint.

• *Include the Development Team in Product Backlog refinement.* The Development Team needs to understand what they are building so that they can meet the business need. Those conversations can start before the Sprint as Product Backlog refinement activities happen. Furthermore, Development Team members will have the knowledge to help break things down into smaller items and in ways that enable more flexibility and creativity in delivering valuable outcomes. Dependencies can be identified and potentially resolved before the PBIs are planned in a Sprint.

In Practice: Using a Scrum Board to Visualize Progress

A Scrum Board is a visual representation of the Sprint Backlog and its progress (see Figure 3-3). Development Teams can keep a physical Scrum Board in their team space so that it's easily accessible and in their line of sight. For remote team members, many digital tools are available that meet this need (both free and paid). The Development Team updates the Scrum Board anytime they have new information about the PBIs they are working on.

PBI	To-Do	In-Progress	Done

Figure 3-3 Sample Scrum Board.

In Figure 3-3, PBIs are captured on the larger cards, and the related breakdown of the activities to complete those PBIs appears in the same row. The columns on the board represent the current state. Be cautious of Scrum Boards that are designed in a way that promotes a waterfall or siloed way of working during the Sprint, such that individuals focus only on "their column." An example would be a "Testing" column that is considered to be "owned" by the people on the Development Team who specialize in testing.

When a Scrum Team effectively uses a Scrum Board, you are likely to hear the following kinds of conversations:

- Team members discussing how to work together on a PBI to get it to "Done" sooner

- Team members asking if they can help on an in-progress PBI rather than picking and starting work on a new PBI

- One team member offering advice to another based on his or her experience working in a certain area of the product

- The team, as a whole, discussing who would like to work on certain PBIs given the current skills and how individuals would like to grow their skills

- Team members expressing concerns about not being able to meet the Sprint Goal and renegotiating scope—what can be removed from the Sprint Backlog, what can be broken down smaller to be more focused on the Sprint Goal

- Team members confirming that new work jeopardizing the Sprint Goal will not be added to the Sprint Backlog but rather directed to the Product Owner

- The team, as a whole, questioning whether work is impeded and discussing what to do to improve flow

- The team, as a whole, discussing how the actionable commitments from the Sprint Retrospective affect how the team is working

- The team, as a whole, recognizing a new dependency and discussing how to resolve it

- The team, as a whole, confirming the DoD has been met when a PBI is moved to "Done"

In Practice: Using a Sprint Burndown to Track Progress

A Sprint Burndown is a chart that tracks PBIs as they are completed, which means that they have met the DoD (see Figure 3-4). Note this chart is different from a Sprint Burndown that tracks tasks or hours, as its focus is on getting PBIs to "Done." Such a chart helps the Scrum Team visualize their work during a Sprint.

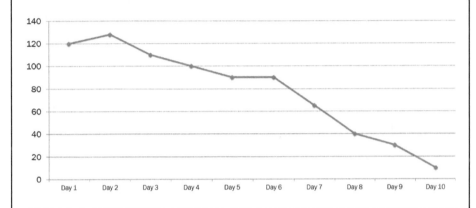

Figure 3-4 Sample Sprint Burndown.

A Sprint Burndown chart can be used in the Sprint Retrospective to talk about the rate at which PBIs are being completed and to identify potential problems and areas for improvement. It helps the Scrum Team ask questions that lead to greater insights during the Sprint Retrospective:

- What happened on specific days when the line flattens that prevented PBIs from being completed? What changes could reduce waste in our process and enable better flow?

- Where did we discover new work? How did we respond to that discovery? What would we do differently in the future?

- What happened on specific days when the line is steeper that helped us complete more PBIs? What can we learn from this moving forward?

Team members might also look at Sprint Burndown charts from previous Sprints and see how the flow has changed over time. Have the improvements they have implemented had the desired effect? Have new challenges arisen? The visualization helps recall details from the past and adapt appropriately.

Limiting Work Items in Progress

When a Development Team is applying the DoD to every PBI, it may also want to limit the number of PBIs in progress. This technique, which applies the Lean Principles to improve flow, helps improve collaboration and learning. For example, a Development Team may set a Work in Progress (WIP) limit of 2 for the "In Progress" column of its Scrum Board. When two PBIs are in progress, a Development Team member who has availability will then focus on helping the team make progress on those two PBIs rather than starting something new.

This approach can be challenging for Development Teams whose members are struggling to figure out how best to apply their skills and knowledge to work collaboratively. Yet they will not likely push beyond that challenge if they don't try. Limiting WIP creates a boundary that forces them to challenge their old ways of working, to be creative in self-organizing around the work, and to be willing to try new things.

As an example, suppose that during the Daily Scrum, Bob states that he wants to start working on a new PBI because the PBIs in flight do not have any front-end design and development needs (his specialty). The Development Team can point to the WIP limit and encourage Bob to take on an activity that contributes to getting an in-progress PBI to "Done," such as running some tests, updating documentation, or pairing with someone.

Why would we want to do this? Well, the short answer is Little's Law.[7] We won't go into a detailed explanation here, but essentially the more things that you work on at any given time (on average), the longer it will take you to finish each of those things (on average). When work takes a long time, people seem to have a natural tendency to start new items as soon as possible so that they can "finish on time," regardless of what is currently in progress. The result is that items end up taking longer to complete due to the many forms of waste created by this situation.

---

7. Read this white paper for more information about how Little's Law applies to Scrum Teams: https://www.scrum.org/resources/littles-law-professional-scrum-kanban.

To get more done overall, you need to focus on doing fewer things at the same time. Fix the impediments that are slowing you down rather than introduce more work into your workflow.

MEASURING AND ANALYZING FLOW

The key to improving a team's process is to create transparency into what is actually happening in the process. Objective data can help identify potential patterns that may be missed when simply relying on observation or trying to remember how the work flowed through the process.

These measures and techniques can help bring transparency to flow within a team's process:

- *Track your cycle time.* You can have multiple "cycles" that you define and measure for your process. To keep things simple, we will define cycle time here as the duration from the time a PBI is started to the time it is ready to release. (Note: Some teams define the endpoint as actual release of the product, especially if that is part of their DoD. Do what makes sense for your team.)
- *Use a Sprint Burndown or throughput chart.* Track the number of PBIs completed per unit of time. Some teams may have a PBI burndown based on size of the PBI (e.g., if they are using story points for sizing). The key here is that the team understands when individual PBIs (not tasks) are getting to "Done."
- *Track your WIP.* Track the total number of PBIs that have started and not yet finished at a point in time. These items are being developed but not yet providing value.
- *Track your blocked PBIs.* When a PBI is started but gets stopped from moving forward somewhere in the process, the PBI is considered blocked. In addition, a team can track how long the item stays in a blocked state and the reason for the blocked state.
- *Pay attention to trends!* The point of capturing these data is to look for trends. Where do the trends point to opportunities for improving the process?

In Practice: Improve Process Transparency and Flow with Kanban

Kanban (n): a strategy for optimizing the flow of stakeholder value through a process that uses a visual, work-in-progress limited pull system.

Flow is the movement of customer value throughout the product development system. Kanban optimizes flow by improving the overall efficiency, effectiveness, and predictability of a process.[8]

Kanban's flow-based perspective and focus on transparency and visualization, combined with the Scrum Framework, can help a team design a process to optimize the means for delivering customer value. Scrum Teams achieve flow optimization by adding the following four practices to their Scrum process:

- Visualization of the workflow

- Limiting WIP

- Active management of work items in progress

- Inspecting and adapting their definition of "workflow"

Kanban emphasizes greater transparency into workflow and identifies a minimum set of flow metrics that are used to actively manage work items in progress and enable flow-oriented inspection and adaptation. It leverages Queueing Theory and Little's Law to make the point that to get more stuff done, you need to work on less. Yep, it sounds crazy, but it is mind-blowingly true.

Ultimately, Kanban enables greater empiricism by providing a few more practices and metrics to help you figure out your best process within the Scrum Framework.[9]

BUILDING IN QUALITY FROM THE BEGINNING

Quality encompasses the user's experience of the product, including how well it balances flexibility, maintainability, efficiency, and responsiveness. Scrum Teams need early and continuous insight into the quality of the product so

---

8. For more information on using Scrum with Kanban, see https://www.scrum.org/resources/kanban-guide-scrum-teams.

9. For more information about Kanban and Scrum, see https://www.scrum.org/resources/blog/understanding-kanban-guide-scrum-teams.

that they can adapt it to meet the customer's needs. In practical terms, this driving force guides teams toward a test-first approach to establish focus on quality from the start.

Taking a test-first approach means the Scrum Team determines its tests before building the solution so that it can get early feedback that the solution under construction works as intended. This results in greater testing coverage as well as higher quality because everything that is built will have also been verified. A number of practices leverage the test-first approach, some of which are combined with automation:

- *Test-Driven Development (TDD)*, in which automated unit tests are created before the code is written to drive the design of the software and force decoupling of dependencies. The work consists of:
  - Writing a "single" unit test describing an aspect of the function
  - Running the test, which should fail because the program lacks that function
  - Writing "just enough" code in the simplest way possible to make the test pass
  - Refactoring the code until it conforms to expected coding standards (as specified in the DoD)

  This process is repeated, creating a set of automated unit tests that grows over time. This set of automated tests can then be run at any time to validate that the product is still working properly.[10]

- *Behavior-Driven Development (BDD)*, which builds on the general principles of TDD and adds ideas from Domain-Driven Design to create automated tests that validate a particular behavior that you want your application to have. Pieces of functionality are built incrementally, guided by the expected behavior. Behavior-driven developers typically use their native language in combination with the language of Domain-Driven Design to describe the purpose and benefit of their code.[11]

---

10. https://www.agilealliance.org/glossary/tdd/
11. https://www.agilealliance.org/glossary/bdd/

- *Acceptance Test–Driven Development (ATDD)*, a collaborative practice in which users and the Development Team define acceptance criteria prior to building any functionality. These tests represent the user's point of view and describe how the system will function. In some cases, the team automates the acceptance tests. This approach places the validation of business functionality as the priority.[12]

AUTOMATION AND "DONE"

Automation is becoming more essential in product development today due to the speed at which many businesses need to deliver value to customers, the complexity and scale of products and systems, and the importance of quality in a world that is becoming more and more dependent on technology. Automating work can seem daunting for teams that do not have experience with it. Automation does require a significant amount of effort, but the benefits are worth the effort:

- Reduced manual effort by team members
- Reduced bottlenecks related to specific skill sets
- Defects found earlier in the delivery cycle
- Reduced chance of human error
- Focusing the skills and energy of team members on tackling new challenges and learning new things

Overall, these benefits contribute to an ability to deliver value faster with higher quality, as well as allowing people to learn faster. If you're building a new product, don't save automation until later. It's easier when you start with a small product and build automation as the product grows—plus you start getting the benefits earlier. And if you are in a situation where a product is already quite large, you'll have to eat the elephant one bite at a time.

Some teams know that they should automate but are always "too busy" to make any progress toward that goal. The solution to this dilemma is to take on less work in a Sprint so as to invest in automation, with the goal of

---

12. https://www.agilealliance.org/glossary/atdd/

creating additional capacity to do more work in the future. A Development Team should work with the Product Owner to make the right trade-offs between reducing progress now so as to achieve greater progress later.

Automation is often addressed in the following order:

1. Version control
2. Automated build
3. Automated test
4. Automated packaging
5. Automated deployment

Automation activities and quality control may be part of a Development Team's DoD. Several different levels of testing may be considered, as illustrated in Figure 3-5. Ultimately, the more levels that are automated, the more certainty you have around the quality you are building into the product.

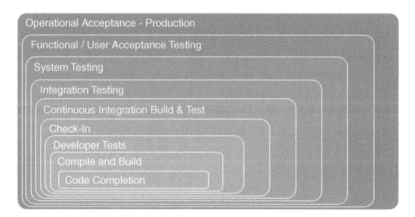

Figure 3-5 Levels of testing.

The Agile Manifesto says that agile teams value working software over comprehensive documentation. This means that the team needs to build and test software. A lot. All of the time, in fact. Ideally, the team needs to build every time it commits a change to the source code repository. But builds are just the starting point—the team also needs to test every time it makes a change. Not just unit tests, but functional tests, regressions tests, performance and scalability tests, all driven from APIs. And not just in simple environments, but ones that look as much like production as possible. When teams do this, they deliver better code.[13]

Technical excellence is an essential capability for Development Teams to grow, and automation practices are a major component of that effort. Continuous Delivery (CD) and the DevOps movement are areas to explore further.[14]

DevOps

There is a lot of confusion about what DevOps is and isn't. Many sources focus on the technical practices, some of which have already been explained (e.g., continuous integration, automated testing, CD, Infrastructure as Code [IaC]). But it is important not to lose sight of the overarching purpose of DevOps: DevOps breaks down barriers between operations and development in pursuit of increased agility.[15]

Code Reviews

In a code review, a Development Team member (or multiple team members) reviews the work done by another team member, so as to provide a quality check. Teams that use this practice often have a checklist of things they are specifically looking at during the code review, which would likely include the DoD. In addition to building quality in, a code review is a great learning opportunity for people to continue to grow their knowledge of the system but also grow their knowledge and skills as developers.[16]

Quality Metrics

Measuring aspects of the product that are indicators of quality helps create transparency so that the Scrum Team can inspect and adapt how quality is

---

13. https://www.scrum.org/resources/blog/what-devops-taught-me-about-agile

14. The book *Continuous Delivery* by Jez Humble and David Farley is a great resource for learning more about broader technical topics, including configuration management, continuous integration, deployment pipelines, managing infrastructure and environments, testing, and managing data.

15. For more information about how agility and DevOps complement each other, see https://www.scrum.org/resources/convergence-scrum-and-devops.

16. For a perspective on why code reviews actually save time, see https://www.atlassian.com/agile/software-development/code-reviews.

impacted by the way in which they build the product and the choices they are making. Some of these metrics are generated by automated tools; others can be tracked manually. Remember that with metrics, the trends are more informative than the specific data points. Moreover, Scrum Teams will want multiple metrics to inspect, given the many variables (both known and unknown) that may influence a metric. Note that these metrics are intended for the Scrum Team's use. To respect and maintain transparency, they should not be used by people outside the team to measure the team's performance, nor should they be incentivized.

Some of the common quality metrics are summarized here:

- *Code coverage metrics* indicate how much of the product's code base is covered by automated tests. This a common data point for teams using TDD. While a high percentage does not guarantee that the code is "written well" and that the tests are maintained, this is a helpful measure for teams.
- *Complexity metrics* help the Development Team understand the degree of maintainability of the code. This kind of quality factor reflects the long-term effectiveness and efficiency of a Scrum Team. Examples of how to measure complexity include cyclomatic complexity, depth of inheritance, class coupling, nesting, and Halstead metrics.
- *Build stability metrics* are a leading indicator of the overall stability of the product. They indicate whether the build process is stable and expose issues related to the code's quality. Build stability can be measured by the number of days since the last red status (build failure) and consecutive red status days.
- *Defect metrics* provide a window into the quality of the product. Bugs are costly to fix in production, and they often interrupt the team's ability to deliver new features and functions. Bugs can have significant impacts on users, ultimately affecting a business's brand, reputation, and bottom line.

In addition to the measures themselves, trends are important, too:

- How many defects are found in production and how many defects are resolved before production, and how is this ratio changing over time?

- How long does it take to fix a production defect, on average, and how is this changing over time?
- What is the average criticality of defects (i.e., what's the cost or impact to the business and customers), and how is this changing over time?
- How many defects recur, and how is this changing over time?
- How long are defects open, and how is this changing over time?

TACKLING TECHNICAL DEBT

Technical debt is deferred work for the product, which often results from decisions made by the Development Team to trade quality for speed. Technical debt can be seen as brittle or difficult-to-change code. Note that taking on technical debt is not necessarily a bad thing—as long as there is a real plan to "pay it off." Just like with financial debt, it can sometimes be a good thing if the return is greater than the interest paid. For example, creating a prototype to test something in the market before investing in a robust backend for the system might be a sound decision. Technical debt must be transparent, as well as the impacts of creating it on the future ability to deliver value.

Examples of technical debt include:

- Lack of automated tests, build, or deployment
- Lack of unit tests
- High code complexity
- Highly coupled code
- Business logic in the wrong places
- Too few acceptance tests
- Duplicated code or modules
- Unreadable names or algorithms

If technical debt in a product accumulates to the point that it becomes difficult to have a releasable Increment of meaningful value by the end of every

Sprint, you need to start paying it off, and quickly. Of course, you want to avoid getting to that point—and the way to do that is to start tackling technical debt sooner, rather than later.[17]

In Practice: Update the DoD to Reflect a Low Tolerance for Technical Debt

It can be helpful to include specific expectations around technical debt in a DoD. What will the Development Team do to avoid creating new technical debt? And what will the Development Team do to resolve existing technical debt?

Here are some examples of things a Development Team may want to address in a DoD related to technical debt:

- What should be refactored?

- How will we leave a module better than we found it (the Boy Scout Rule)?

- When we encounter technical debt in building the Increment, what will we do? What technical debt will we look for and resolve as we build?

- What will we do with technical debt that remains unresolved?

A Development Team's DoD is a form of a working agreement, so it is important to make explicit how technical debt will be both prevented and managed. This agreement both helps team members hold each other accountable for high quality standards and makes quality more transparent to stakeholders.

MAKING TECHNICAL DEBT TRANSPARENT

Adding technical debt to the Product Backlog will make it transparent to the Scrum Team and stakeholders. This step also enables the Product Owner to make better decisions about ordering the work. If you do, be sure to clearly capture the value of resolving the technical debt in business terms. What will the business gain by resolving this technical debt? What is it costing the business to not resolve this technical debt? How are users being impacted by not resolving this technical debt?

---

17. To explore the topic of technical debt further, watch this Scrum.org webinar by Mark Noneman, *Dealing with Technical Debt: Avoiding Technical Bankruptcy*: https://www.scrum.org/resources/dealing-technical-debt.

Here are some examples of capturing value in business terms. Consider adding data reflecting existing quality issues or expected efficiency gains based on history for the specific product.

- Refactor so there are fewer pathways through the code, reducing time to test by 30 percent.
- Apply consistent naming and structural conventions, allowing team members to be more effective and more efficient when building new features and fixing issues.
- Centralize the business logic for Feature X, making it easier to update the business logic in the future, and reducing the likelihood of bugs. In the last 4 months, we have had 24 bugs that directly impacted customers and resulted in loss of $100,000 profit.
- Refactor Feature Y, increasing the performance of the system by 35 percent, and resulting in a transaction time improvement of 2.5 seconds.
- Refactor Feature Z so that, now the customer viability has been proven, we will be able to scale the solution to a broader user base, leading to more revenue.

In Practice: Treat Technical Debt Like Credit Card Debt

Stop creating it. And start paying it back, a little bit every Sprint. If technical debt has gotten so bad that the team finds it quite challenging to deliver a "Done" Increment with significant value to the business, the Scrum Team should have a discussion about this issue—and determine if it is time to cut up the credit card and start paying a little more than interest payments every Sprint.

The Development Team can help the Product Owner understand the criticality of addressing the problem of technical debt and negotiate an amount of time to set aside in upcoming Sprints for PBIs related to technical debt. The Product Owner can help stakeholders understand the value they are getting from resolving these issues.

This approach should continue to be inspected and adapted to understand the benefits gained and to adjust the amount of time spent resolving technical debt as appropriate.

MAKING TECHNICAL DEBT "REPAYMENT" VISIBLE

If a product has a significant amount of technical debt to pay back, consider creating a visible progress indicator for the team. This step starts with the Scrum Team setting an initial goal or perhaps multiple goals. Team members can then create an information radiator that tracks their progress toward paying back the technical debt during each Sprint.

Figure 3-6 shows an example using a thermometer as a metaphor and progress indicator. Perhaps the Scrum Team sets a goal of resolving a certain amount of technical debt over the course of several Sprints, and the thermometer helps them to celebrate the small gains made every Sprint. Another approach is a burndown chart showing the total amount of technical debt known (i.e., transparent in the Product Backlog) and tracking the trend over time as technical debt gets resolved, uncovered, or perhaps created intentionally.

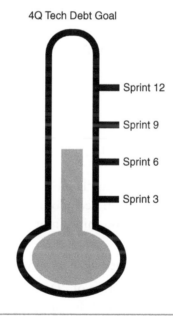

Figure 3-6 Visualizing technical debt can provide motivation to do something about it.

SUMMARY

Getting to "Done" is essential to delivering value while controlling risk and managing complexity. As a Scrum Team forms a stronger foundation, it will naturally be in a position to evolve the team process to more effectively deliver a high-quality, high-value product. There are no "best practices" in Scrum, so teams must continually examine what they are doing, why they are doing it, and what benefits they are (or are no longer) getting. Technology and business change all the time, so teams must look for what's coming next and what they need to do differently to meet new needs, stay ahead of the competition, and delight customers.

The flexibility provided by the minimal boundaries of the Scrum Framework opens up many possibilities to unleash the creativity of collaborative teams. They can navigate the possibilities by always seeking better transparency into their process and its effects on outcomes, and by frequently inspecting and adapting the team process based on these insights. Teams should minimally consider how well they are using a definition of "Done" and Sprint Goals, how work flows through their process, and which quality practices and measures are needed.

CALL TO ACTION

Consider these questions with your team:

- Are you reliably getting to "Done" at least by the end of every Sprint? If not, what has the team been doing about it? Otherwise, where are there opportunities to do things more effectively with higher quality and greater joy?
- How do the Scrum values show up in your team process?
- How robust is the definition of "Done"? How has it evolved over time, and what opportunities are there for improvement?
- How are Sprint Goals being used throughout the Sprint?

- How much transparency do you have to the way work flows through the Sprint? Where do you need more?
- How is quality trending for the product?
- How much technical debt is in the product? Is it increasing or decreasing?
- Where does the team need to grow knowledge and skills to create a releasable Increment of appropriate quality sooner?
- Which challenges are hurting the team most right now? Identify one or two experiments to help evolve the team process and more effectively get to "Done." For each experiment, be sure to identify the desired impacts and how you will measure them.

IMPROVING VALUE DELIVERED

Producing a "Done" Product Increment isn't the end of the journey—it's merely the start of the learning journey to deliver more value. A Scrum Team now has the capability to measure the value they deliver and to use empiricism to improve the value that customers experience.

WHAT IS VALUE?

The term *value* is used many times in the Scrum Guide. The first time this term is used is in the definition of Scrum: "delivering products of the highest possible value." It is an interesting experiment to ask people how they define "value." It is actually difficult to define what value means without using the words "value" or "valuable." Value is, ultimately, determined by customer experiences.

These questions can help you determine whether you are delivering value:

- Are your customers happy? Do you help them achieve outcomes that they find important?
- Is that happiness reflected in ways that can be profitably monetized?

- Are you adding or shedding customers?
- How quickly can you deliver a new idea to a customer and measure the result?
- Are your employees happy?

Not-for-profit and social enterprises don't have concerns about profitably monetizing customer outcomes. Even so, they are still concerned with customer outcomes—although they may use names like "citizens" or "clients" instead of "customers." Some for-profit enterprises are also mission-driven, but missions can be described in terms of achieving a set of outcomes for a group of people, as in the following examples:

- Increasing local employment
- Improving the well-being of a community
- Reducing negative ecological or environmental impacts

Noted management consultant, educator, and author Peter Drucker observed, "If you can't measure it, you can't improve it." The same is true of value: Producing and delivering "Done" Product Increments is not enough; you have to measure the value you are delivering to improve it.

DELIVERING FASTER IS A GOOD START, BUT NOT ENOUGH

While many organizations turn to Scrum to "deliver faster," once they start delivering to customers and measuring the results, they discover that the real benefit of Scrum is getting feedback sooner to drive faster improvement. In fact, if faster delivery alone could solve the problems that organizations face in meeting customer needs, a traditional approach with many very small releases would suffice.

The problem is that, to paraphrase John Wanamaker, more than half of our ideas deliver no value; we just don't know which half.[1] To improve your ability

---

1. John Wanamaker (1838–1922), a wealthy department store owner, famously observed that "Half the money I spend on advertising is wasted; the trouble is, I don't know which half."

to deliver value, you have to not only improve the speed at which you deliver value, but also measure what you deliver to determine its value, and you must use that feedback to improve the value you deliver in the next release.

Studies have shown that 65 percent of features are rarely or never used (see Figure 4-1).[2] In a similar vein, a 2017 article in the *Harvard Business Review* stated that "the vast majority of [new ideas] fail in experiments, and even experts often misjudge which ones will pay off. At Google and Bing, only about 10% to 20% of experiments generate positive results. At Microsoft as a whole, one-third prove effective, one-third have neutral results, and one-third have negative results."[3]

Standish Group, Features and Function Usage

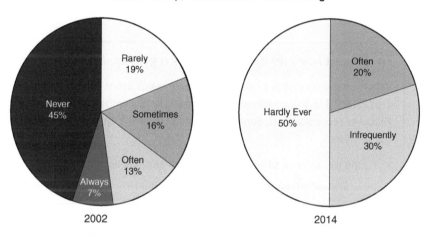

Figure 4-1 Most features are rarely or never used.

Value is easy to understand when measured in terms of revenue, income, and direct costs, but not all value is monetary in nature. Market share growth rate, diversity of the customer base, customer satisfaction, employee satisfaction, and employee turnover rate are also important measures of value. Likewise, ease of use and ease of product adoption can be important measures that inform product improvements.

---

2. *The Professional Product Owner: Leveraging Scrum as a Competitive Advantage* by Don McGreal and Ralph Jocham (Addison-Wesley, 2018), part of the Professional Scrum Series from Scrum.org.
3. https://hbr.org/2017/09/the-surprising-power-of-online-experiments

PRODUCT VALUE AND THE SCRUM TEAM

In Scrum, the Product Owner is accountable for maximizing the outcomes that the product will deliver to customers, thereby maximizing the value realized by the organization.

This focus on value and outcomes represents a change for organizations in which output has historically been the measure of success. Output measures things that are produced or consumed, such as features delivered or story points. Output is easy to measure, but it is of only secondary importance: The number of features delivered is irrelevant if none of those features improves the lives or capabilities of the customer. Features delivered matters only in consideration of profitability or time-to-market, but if they produced nothing of value then they are simply waste.

In Practice: Measuring Progress and Success

When people talk about "status" or "progress," listen for the mindset driving the discussion. If it is just about percent complete, number of features built, or red/yellow/green status, ask some powerful questions that bring focus to the value of the product:

- Could we achieve all of these measures and still be unsuccessful?
- How are we validating assumptions about the user needs or the market demand?
- What are we learning about value? How is this guiding our product decisions?
- What has changed with our users or our competitive environment since we began this initiative?

Too often, "percent complete" and similar discussions hide an assumption that everything on the "wish list" is important and valuable. The aforementioned studies prove that they are not. Instead of worrying about whether everything will get done, focus discussions on how you can more quickly test assumptions about value to reduce waste and increase the value that you deliver.

The Scrum Team determines its process within the Scrum Framework. This process includes defining value, delivering value, and measuring value.

Although the Product Owner remains accountable, it is likely that a Product Owner needs help. The Product Owner needs input from stakeholders, including customers, users, and Development Team members. The Product Owner also depends on the Development Team to actually deliver value, so it's important that those team members understand the outcomes that customers seek to better inform decisions.[4]

The Product Backlog creates transparency into the relative importance of the work that the Product Owner believes will maximize value delivered. When it's used most effectively, it forms the foundation for a dialogue with the rest of the Scrum Team as well as stakeholders, about what is valuable.

USING THE PRODUCT VISION TO ENLIVEN TEAM PURPOSE, FOCUS, AND IDENTITY

The Product Vision expresses the *raison d'etre* of the product—who it is for, and what it hopes to do for them. It is important when defining and funding the product, but it also has value in bringing purpose and focus to the Scrum Team and helping them form their identity. Returning to this vision periodically is a useful way to remind everyone on the team why the team exists.[5] Various related techniques help the team shape and reinforce their identity:

- *Product value.* A clear understanding of value helps a team understand the why behind their work and how to validate whether their work is contributing value. Knowing the value in a tangible way (e.g., revenue,

---

4. For a much deeper dive into defining products and how to better understand what customers will find valuable, we recommend Scrum.org's Professional Scrum Product Owner class: https://www.scrum.org/courses/professional-scrum-product-owner-training. If you can't make it to a class, or even if you can, we also recommend *The Professional Scrum Product Owner* by McGreal and Jocham, part of Scrum.org's Professional Scrum Series.

5. For more information on creating a strong product vision, see *The Professional Product Owner: Leveraging Scrum as a Competitive Advantage* by McGreal and Jocham.

market share, customer satisfaction) goes a long way toward instilling a sense of purpose.

- *Personas.* Personas help a team understand users and customers better, so as to develop empathy for them. This ultimately helps team members see the purpose in their work and create better solutions. Some teams post their persona descriptions around their work environment as a continual reminder of the people they are working to help.[6]

- *Product Roadmap.* A Product Roadmap is a visual representation of the high-level plan intended to help a team see the direction of the product over time. The more a roadmap focuses on business objectives and business value, the more it provides a solid purpose.

In Practice: Enlivening the Product Vision

It is easy for the Product Vision to be defined early in a product's life cycle, but then become forgotten in the pursuit of individual releases. Products change over time, and they can do so either mindfully or accidentally. Feature creep and other forms of harmful scope expansion are often caused by the lack of focus that results from a confused or unfocused Product Vision. Consider these ways to keep the Product Vision keenly tuned:

1. *Involve a broader community.* Your stakeholders and your Development Team likely have valuable perspectives and ideas. And by including others, you help them feel heard, which is likely to increase their commitment to and understanding of the Product Vision. Using the Product Vision to engage in periodic discussions of who the product should serve and what it should do for them is a good way to evolve it in mindful, and not accidental ways.

2. *Evolve it based on new information.* The initial Product Vision is a starting point, based on assumptions and guesses, many of which will be correct but some of which will prove wrong. You will need to inspect, adapt, and evolve the Product Vision based on new information.

---

6. For more information on personas, see http://gamestorming.com/empathy-mapping/ and https://www.romanpichler.com/blog/10-tips-agile-personas/.

3. *Keep it focused.* Successful products have a clear focus; the teams building them know who they are serving and how. Poor products try to do a little something for everyone, but not very much for anyone.

4. *Constantly reinforce it.* In the words of Professional Scrum Trainer Don McGreal, "Be annoying about it." Product Owners should look for opportunities to reinforce the Product Vision, as well as validate alignment to the Product Vision. Product Owners can bring the physical manifestation of the Product Vision to Sprint Reviews or other discussions with stakeholders and the Development Team (e.g., the Product Box[7] or a poster of the elevator pitch).[8]

MEASURING VALUE

Scrum Teams can measure the value they deliver in a variety of ways, and different kinds of value will need to be measured in different ways, ranging from very general about the product as a whole to highly specific about certain PBIs. In reality, you will probably need all of the following kinds of measures at different times:

General measures of customer happiness:

- Net Promoter Score
- Revenue or profitability per customer
- Repeat customer business
- Reduction in total cost of ownership
- Improved conversion rates
- Growth in number of customers or users
- Customer referrals

---

7. For more on the Product Box technique, see https://www.innovationgames.com/product-box/.
8. For examples of elevator pitches, see https://strategypeak.com/elevator-pitch-examples/.

Achievement of business goals:

- Market share
- Aggregate revenue or profit
- Cost to obtain a new customer
- Reduction in cycle time, reductions in inventory on hand, cost savings, or increases in market share

Specific measures of customer results:

- Time saved for the customer to achieve a goal
- Frequency of feature usage
- Duration of feature usage
- Number of customers or users using a feature
- Transaction completion/abandon rates

In Practice: Using Several Measures to Diagnose Product Problems

The preceding lists are not exhaustive, but rather illustrate that different kinds of measures can be used to quantify value in different ways. In most cases, one measure will trigger questions that require other measures to explain. For example, a general decline in the Net Promoter Score or customer referrals suggests that customers have become less happy with the product. When you start measuring what users are actually doing with the product, you might find that some new feature that you introduced has made the product harder to use, leading to the general dissatisfaction that you measured earlier.

Scrum Teams can improve their measures of value in a variety of ways:

- *Involve others.* Just as with a Product Vision, your stakeholders and your Development Team likely have valuable perspectives and ideas. Also, by including others, you help them feel heard, which is likely to increase their commitment to and understanding of product value.

- *Make measures visible.* Measures should be transparent to all stakeholders and the Development Team. Consider creating a dashboard of value metrics for the product.

- *Talk about measures and results in Sprint Reviews.* As features and functions are being demonstrated to attendees, speak to the value expected and how it will be known if it is achieved.
- *Relate measures and results back to business goals.* This comes back to creating alignment and helps provide the rationale for how you are defining value. And if business goals change, then that can be a good indicator that you need to inspect and possibly adapt your value definitions and measures.

FOCUSING PBIS ON USER OUTCOMES

Understanding user needs and desires is key to understanding what is valuable and why. Scrum Teams can apply a number of techniques to understand users better. In particular, two techniques often combined to help Scrum Teams better understand and focus on users are personas/outcomes and User Stories.

Personas and Outcomes

A *persona* is a fictional character created to represent a user or customer type that might use a product in a similar way. Personas are often created through market research data and customer interviews. They bring the person to life (so to speak) by painting a picture with information related to demographics, lifestyle, goals, and reasons for using the product. Using personas helps the Scrum Team achieve focus by helping them get very specific about who they are targeting with a particular PBI.

An *outcome* is some condition or goal that a person matching the persona would like to achieve. Understanding these goals helps a Scrum Team achieve focus by clearly articulating what the user or customer would like to achieve.

Using personas and outcomes has the following principal benefits:

- Help the people building the products empathize more with the users and their needs
- Help identify user pain points and creative solutions
- Help create focus while still being able to see the whole

Personas and outcomes are antidotes to features that don't have clear objectives or a clear target audience. Personas also help avoid vague discussions about "the user," because no product has a single homogenous kind of user; instead, people use the same product in very different ways to achieve very different outcomes.

In Practice: Using Impact Maps to Gain Better Product Insights

Impact mapping can be a useful technique for connecting PBIs back to the goals they are intended to meet.[9] You can use a modified impact map to connect the business goal you are trying to achieve to the *personas* that you will serve, the *outcomes* you hope to help them achieve, the *impacts* to your organization if you meet that outcome, and the *PBIs* that you will deliver in the product to achieve those outcomes (see Figure 4-2).

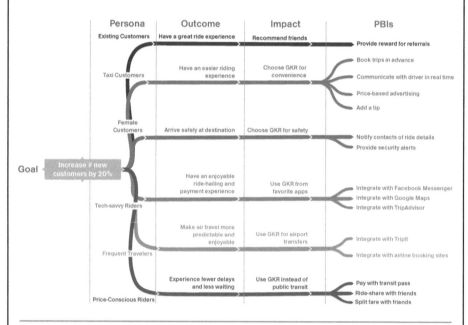

Figure 4-2 An extended impact map helps connect PBIs back to goals.

---

9. For a description of a useful extension of impact mapping, see https://www.scrum.org/resources/blog/extending-impact-mapping-gain-better-product-insights.

In the example in Figure 4-2, the organization—a company that is entering the ride-sharing service market—would like to increase the number of new customers by 20 percent. To do so, it needs to appeal to many different kinds of potential riders, each represented by a different *persona*. Each persona has different *outcomes* that it would like to achieve. The company believes that by satisfying specific outcomes, it will achieve certain *impacts*, or results for the company, and it believes that delivering certain PBIs will help the company do that.

Impact maps can be used in a variety of ways. In the context of Product Backlog refinement, they help the Scrum Team think about how each PBI will provide some outcome. Impact maps also help the Product Owner envision who the product serves, what those different kinds of users or stakeholders would like to achieve by using the product, and how the organization will benefit from helping customers achieve specific outcomes.

In Practice: Expressing PBIs as Hypotheses or Experiments

Hypothesis-Driven Development (HDD) is a way of expressing PBIs in a way that makes the persona, outcome, measurement, and expected result explicit.[10] The discipline of HDD helps Scrum Teams to frame hypotheses and experiments and to be mindful about how they will know whether a hypothesis (or assumption) is true. This encourages everyone to think about not only what they are trying to accomplish, but also how they will measure it.[11] Figure 4-3 provides an example of one way to express a hypothesis.

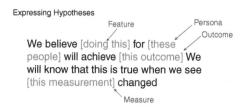

Figure 4-3 Explicitly expressing hypotheses can help teams uncover unstated assumptions.

---

10. Scrum.org's Professional Scrum with User Experience Course (https://www.scrum.org/courses/professional-scrum-user-experience-training) teaches how to integrate modern UX practices with Scrum, based on the book *Lean UX* by Jeff Gothelf and Josh Seiden (O'Reilly Media, 2016).

11. For more on Scrum and HDD, see https://www.scrum.org/resources/blog/scrum-and-hypothesis-driven-development.

User Stories

User Stories are both widely used and widely misused. Their original intent was to serve as a *placeholder* or token for a conversation about how someone would use the product to achieve some outcome. When they stray from that reminder to have a conversation and become a format for documenting PBIs, they can become utter nonsense, particularly when used to express technical requirements or constraints. To keep this from happening, focus on the 3 Cs of User Stories:[12]

- The *Card*, which is simply a reminder to have Conversations. It should have a simple, minimal format that fits on an index card (or a sticky note) and may consist of nothing more than "Talk to Mary about how accounts are settled at the end of a billing period."
- The *Conversation*, which is the actual discussion about the topic mentioned on the card.
- The *Confirmation*, which are the actual tests that prove it works.[13]

In Practice: Common Product Backlog Item Pitfalls

Regardless of the format that your PBIs take (personas and outcomes, User Stories, or something else), beware of these common traps:

1. *Assuming that PBIs must follow a set format.* The commonly used format for User Stories is not the original format, nor is it required. It may be helpful for your Scrum Team to use a format, but they don't have to fight to fit a PBI into that format. Write what makes sense. After all, the Card is just a reminder to have a Conversation.

2. *Not being clear on the user or customer the PBI benefits.* If you are writing over and over again, "As a user" at the beginning of a User Story, you are not helping create focus and understanding of the user for whom you are designing a feature or function. As noted in #1, you don't have to always use this format, but you should have a shared understanding of the users and customers for your product.

---

12. https://www.agilealliance.org/glossary/user-stories/
13. If you want to apply User Stories as an effective Product Backlog refinement technique, we recommend Mike Cohn's book *User Stories Applied* (Addison-Wesley Professional, 2004).

3. *Not clarifying the value.* Often PBIs will state a desired feature, function, or capability, but precisely why that item is desired is not clear. When there isn't a shared understanding of why you are building something, it is possible that alternative solutions to the problem will not be discussed. This misses an opportunity to maximize value.

4. *Treating the PBI as a contract.* The Product Backlog is not just the "agile version" of a traditional software requirements document. PBIs are open to change. Consider the User Story technique: It is meant to represent a customer's needs, not just document them. User Stories are to be elaborated, even during the work of building it.

5. *Including implementation details.* PBIs should be focused on the "what" rather than the "how." If you make implementation decisions too early, you may limit your options. You may also create waste by detailing things that are likely to change when implementation actually occurs.

IMPROVING VALUE DELIVERED DURING THE SPRINT

As the Development Team works on PBIs during a Sprint, their understanding of the value that the PBIs will deliver continues to improve as they learn more, through conversations, through stakeholder feedback, and even from real customers or users if the team is releasing a product during the Sprint. (Yes, this is possible!)[14] A PBI is never "locked down" or "finalized" until it is actually "Done." This includes the details of both what is being built and how it is being built. If members of a Development Team are collaborating with one another, as well as with the Product Owner, they can constantly ask questions related to value and let this drive their decision-making process. For example:

• A Scrum Team chooses to split a PBI to focus on the most valuable acceptance criteria for the user functionality required now, which allows the lower-value piece to be reprioritized at a later time based on a consideration of other desired functions.

• When seeing a new capability implemented in the product, the Product Owner provides guidance on how to make it more prominent to the target users.

---

14. For a deeper perspective on releasing during a Sprint, see https://www.scrum.org/resources/blog/myth-3-scrum-releases-are-done-only-end-sprint.

- The Development Team sees alternative ways to increase user conversion, which is the stated value of the PBI they are building. They bring these options to the Product Owner, and they negotiate a change to the scope to better meet the business need while still delivering a "Done" Increment in the Sprint.

INSPECTING AND ADAPTING BASED ON FEEDBACK

Once you've released the product or demonstrated the product to stakeholders, you will have empirical data that you can use to confirm (or reject) your hypotheses. One data point in time usually doesn't tell you much, but trends over time will show you whether you are getting better or worse in a particular dimension. And, remember, you may need different measures to really understand what is going on.

For example, you might have very happy customers who love your product, but no measures of their happiness will tell you why people don't buy your product. If you want to expand your market share, you will need to measure more than the *current value* delivered by the product—that is, you will also need to understand which factors prevent you from realizing the full market potential of your product.[15]

As you are analyzing the value trends, consider what changes you released and when and how they may have impacted value. Consider what factors are beyond your control (e.g., a big decline in the stock market could impact users' decisions even though you've implemented new features you expected to increase sales).

LEARNING AS VALUE

Sometimes the value lies in the learning. This process may or may not be data-driven, but it can be helpful to be explicit about learning as the value.

---

15. Scrum.org has developed a framework for understanding how to measure value and improve your ability to deliver value called Evidence-Based Management. The two dimensions of value are Current Value, referring to the value realized by current customers of your product, and Unrealized Value, meaning the potential value that you could deliver to all potential customers, but do not deliver today. For more information, see https://www.scrum.org/resources/evidence-based-management.

For example, a Scrum Team may want to learn which of two technology services will be easy both to implement and to enhance, while also meeting the business needs. In another example, a Scrum Team might want to learn which user experience is most likely to lead to a purchase.

EFFECTIVE SPRINT REVIEWS INCLUDE VALUE REALIZED

Recall that the outcome of a Sprint Review is adaptation of the Product Backlog. In addition to stakeholder feedback on the Product Increment and overall market trends, actual value data and trends give you even more empirical data to guide Product Backlog decisions.

Make your actual value measures transparent. Get input on what stakeholders see in the trends and how they think it should inform adaptation.

GATHERING STAKEHOLDER FEEDBACK

How you approach gathering input from stakeholders will depend on many factors, including, but not limited to, the complexity of your product, the number of stakeholders you have, the diversity of stakeholder types and their needs, and where your stakeholders are located. You often need to pay special attention to stakeholders to gather the most valuable information from them. While they are usually quite expert in some area of interest, you might need to steer their attention toward the things about which you need feedback. Keep in mind that Sprint Reviews are not the only time Product Owners can get input from and collaborate with stakeholders. You will get more from stakeholder collaboration sessions in general, and Sprint Reviews in particular, if you can focus stakeholders' participation in the following ways:

- *Be explicit about what you are reviewing and what feedback you are looking for.* Having a simple but explicit agenda for feedback sessions helps everyone focus.
- *Make feedback sessions active, and encourage participation.* People thrive on activity. Conversely, sitting passively, listening to someone drone on about features, functions, and capabilities, is often boring for participants. Organizing sessions in ways that force people to move will keep them more

engaged, which in turn often saves time. Also, people are more likely to feel heard if they physically participated in an activity.

- *Enable stakeholders to collaborate with each other.* Stakeholders can learn from each other. Not everyone shares the same perspective, and sometimes this results in conflicts that could be resolved if stakeholders understand each other's perspectives.

- *Make collaboration visible.* It is easier to discuss a wide range of ideas when we can see them in a physical space and easily add, update, and move information. In addition, this approach creates transparency into what we are trying to accomplish and what we learned together by the end. It is also helpful to have that vision and definition of value visible to keep things focused.

- *Break into smaller groups during a session.* Smaller groups of people interested in particular topics are usually more effective than large group discussions. Allow time for them to have smaller group discussions and bring their results back to the group.

- *Introduce techniques that encourage relative value comparisons.* It is easy to get bogged down in details, especially when discussing which PBIs are more valuable than others. By comparing value relatively (i.e., Item X is more valuable than Item Y but less valuable than Item Z), we can get enough information quickly.[16]

Summary

Scrum is not designed to help you build and release more "stuff." Instead, Scrum helps you maximize the value you create for your customers, and therefore for your organization, by frequently delivering a product, measuring the results, and then learning and adapting so as to wring more value out of the product.

In this chapter, we explored how empiricism, an agile mindset, and teamwork guide you in fiercely tackling difficult product value questions. You must have

---

16. For specific facilitation techniques to gather input about relative value to help with Product Backlog ordering, see *The Professional Product Owner* by McGreal and Jocham, p. 213.

transparency into value, and you must engage in frequent enough inspections of the actual value realized that you can keep moving in the best direction. Just like the complexity and unpredictability inherent in building a releasable product, figuring out what to build entails some complexity and unpredictability. Scrum provides the minimal level of empiricism, and the Scrum Team needs to determine their process within the Scrum Framework. This process includes how you enable value emergence, measure actual value, and adapt to new information and the changing environment.

The Product Owner is the single person accountable for optimizing value. An empirical Product Owner will engage and empower others to support them in achieving this goal. A strong Product Owner will foster a product mindset across the organization and paint the bigger picture, creating alignment within the Development Team and among stakeholders on the direction of the product and how value is defined. The Product Owner works collaboratively with the Development Team and stakeholders to enable value emergence iteratively and incrementally, guided by the learning from measuring actual value.

CALL TO ACTION

Consider these questions with your team:

- How well is the Product Vision understood by the Development Team and stakeholders?
- Where do you need more transparency into desired outcomes and value assumptions?
- What value measures would help you make more informed decisions about what is in the Product Backlog and its order? How frequently would you need to inspect those data?
- How does the Development Team collaborate with the Product Owner or relevant stakeholders during the Sprint?
- How much feedback and new insights come out of the Sprint Review or other collaborative sessions with stakeholders?

- Do stakeholders focus on value delivery as the key measure of success? What conversations can you have to help shift the focus in the right direction?

- What challenges are hurting the most right now? Identify one or two experiments to help improve understanding and measurement of value. For each experiment, be sure to identify the desired impacts and how you will measure them.

IMPROVING 5 PLANNING

Taking an empirical approach to delivering complex products in an uncertain and rapidly changing world requires empirical planning. This means that in planning activities, aim to:

- Enable transparency to progress
- Set realistic expectations
- Minimize waste while maximizing value
- Harness change and new learnings for competitive advantage
- Have open and honest discussions about the unpredictability and complexity inherent in product development

Business leaders and customers will still—and should—ask questions such as "When will it be ready?" and "How much will it cost?" When you work empirically, your answers to these questions will reflect likelihoods and probabilities rather than commitments and certainties. You cannot perfectly plan complex work, but rather must remain open to change and new knowledge. Even within the time horizon of a Sprint, there are complexities, unknowns, and possibilities for change.

There are four key things a Scrum Team should get out of its planning activities:

1. Establish a common set of understandings from which emergence, adaptation, and collaboration can occur (agile mindset, empiricism, teamwork).

2. Establish expectations that progress will be measured against (empiricism).

3. Convince a source of funding that the ROI of an initiative is worthwhile (agile mindset).

4. Help people involved in the value delivery process make better decisions (empiricism, agile mindset).

Planning and forecasting encompass a wide range of topics. In this chapter, we will focus on illuminating the following concepts for planning and provide additional resources to explore specific tactics:

• How Scrum Teams plan empirically and get the most benefits from Product Backlog refinement

• How Scrum Teams plan effectively to create a "Done" Increment of sufficient value during every Sprint, while incorporating learning and continuous improvement

• How Scrum Teams can approach release planning without having to plan many Sprints in advance

PLANNING WITH A PRODUCT MINDSET

A product mindset helps Scrum Teams and organizations focus on delivering valuable outcomes rather than just concentrating on the quantity of output.[1] It is easier to understand this approach when we compare it with a project mindset.

According to the Project Management Institute (PMI), a project is a temporary endeavor undertaken to create a unique product, service, or result.[2] The two key points in this definition are that a project has a

---

1. For a more complete description of the differences between a project mindset and a product mindset, see https://www.scrum.org/resources/blog/project-mindset-or-product-mindset.

2. https://www.pmi.org/about/learn-about-pmi/what-is-project-management

beginning and an end date (which creates boundaries around scope and resources), and it is not repeatable.

When you think about Scrum, you could look at every Sprint as a project. The Sprint has start and end dates, and the Scrum Team produces a unique releasable Increment during that span. Or you could consider a subset of the Product Backlog as a project that encompasses multiple Sprints and achieves a value proposition or business goal through delivery of multiple Increments. The point we are trying to make here is that these concepts are interwoven. However, the challenge arises when you consider how success is often measured.

MEASURING SUCCESS

In our experience, project success is traditionally measured by answering these three questions:

- Did you deliver all of the scope?
- Did you do it within budget?
- Did you do it on time?

These questions are derived from the Project Management Triangle, also known as the Iron Triangle or the Triple Constraint, illustrated in Figure 5-1.

Figure 5-1 Iron Triangle of project management.

The problem with only using these variables as the measure of success is that doing so leaves out valuable outcomes. How do you know if the investment is worth it? How do you know if you need to change direction or if you can stop investing sooner? And even if an organization does measure the ROI against the original business case for the project, that usually happens after the project has completed, so it is too late to matter. Besides, business cases are themselves just educated guesses whose assumptions need to be tested using empiricism.

PLANNING EMPIRICALLY

"A plan is simply a guess you wrote down."[3] Instead of doing a lot of analysis and estimation up-front to create a long-term detailed plan, take an empirical approach to planning. Empiricism says learning comes from doing. You plan a little, actually do that work, and then inspect the results, asking "What assumptions have we validated? What did we learn?" Based on new information, you adapt your plan accordingly. By modifying your plans based on new information, you minimize the risk of complex work in an unpredictable and changing world.

Planning empirically requires transparency. The agile mindset helps remind us that the only measure of progress is a working product. Completing some "activities" doesn't deliver any value if there is no working product. There is no such thing as 85 percent complete when it comes to a "Done" Increment, or any other complex work. That type of "status update" is often a wild guess at best, and sometimes an effort to avoid difficult questions and conversations. Furthermore, when organizations focus on meeting a schedule and/or budget, they discourage transparency and openness to change and learnings. This actually increases—rather than reduces—risk.

The agile mindset also reminds us to seek to maximize value and reduce waste. Consider how much waste is created when you frequently update long-term detailed plans. How much waste is created by change control processes that create a lot of work to incorporate new information into your plan? What value is potentially lost or delayed when people feel the burden of a heavy change control process and choose to just "stick with the plan and hope for the best"? When teams are pushed to meet a deadline, quality is

---

3. https://m.signalvnoise.com/planning-is-guessing/

often sacrificed. Ultimately, this costs you in the longer term because it damages your ability to deliver future value.

Staying grounded in empiricism and the agile mindset will help maintain a focus on a product mindset as a Scrum Team plans the work for the product, from the shorter-term to the longer-term planning horizons. This grounding will also remind everyone that the less history a Scrum Team has (i.e., empirical data) and the further into the future the forecast stretches, the wider the range of unknowns, complexities, and likelihood for change will be.

In Practice: Empiricism Reduces Uncertainty by Taking Action, Not by Planning More

Traditional project management approaches suggest that making more detailed plans reduces risk, but more planning actually just delays confronting risk by making more assumptions. This is why so many traditional projects fail. For example, describing a detailed architecture for a product does nothing to tell you whether that architecture will actually work. The best way to understand whether something will work is to build a critical subset of the solution and try it out.

This point is even more true for ideas about what consumers will like. The only way to know for sure whether customers will like your product is to actually deliver something minimally usable, sometimes called the Minimum Viable Product (MVP).[4]

The cone of uncertainty[5] is a project management model that expresses the reduction in uncertainty of outcomes as an organization gathers more information. At the start of a release, uncertainty about what to build and how to build it can be quite high. Plans will be quite "rough"—perhaps nothing more than desired outcomes, some possible features and functions to achieve those outcomes, and a rough idea of desired release dates based on market conditions. As the Scrum Team completes Sprints, they gather information and refine the Product Backlog, and they develop a better understanding of how much work they will need to do to achieve the desired outcomes. The Product Owner can trust the empirical process, knowing that something of value will be "Done" at least by the end of every Sprint. In turn, the new information and new learnings will guide the Product Owner in deciding to continue forward, adapt the direction, or stop investing.

---

4. For more information on the Minimum Viable Product concept, see https://www.agilealliance.org/glossary/mvp.

5. https://www.construx.com/books/the-cone-of-uncertainty

CREATING ALIGNMENT

Planning is only effective when there is alignment to value delivery in the organization. Alignment is about everyone moving in the same direction. You can visualize planning product delivery as peeling the layers of an onion, as illustrated in Figure 5-2.

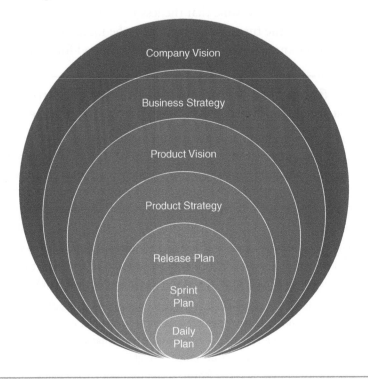

Figure 5-2 Planning product delivery requires alignment through the various levels in an organization.

The Scrum Framework directly addresses the two innermost (i.e., shorter-term) levels of planning. The Daily Scrum is a plan for the next 24 hours to make progress toward the Sprint Goal. The Sprint Goal is created in Sprint Planning and is informed by an ordered Product Backlog. The Product Owner's strategy for moving toward a Product Vision is essentially reflected in the Product Backlog. Finally, to maximize value, the Product Vision and strategy must be aligned with the organization's business strategy.

Each layer represents a different planning horizon in the context of the product and how it fits into the direction of the larger organization. Looking at the bigger picture, these questions are likely to come up:

- How far in advance should you plan, and at what level of detail for each layer?
- How frequently should you inspect and adapt your plans at each layer?
- Who should be involved in planning for the outer layers that go beyond the Scrum Team?

The answer to all of these questions is "It depends!"

It depends on the complexity of your product and its relationship to the greater organization, as well as the environment in which it is used. Consider how the planning cycles in your organization enable empirical planning and alignment between the bigger picture business objectives and the work being done by the Scrum Team.

PRODUCT BACKLOG REFINEMENT

Product Backlog refinement is an activity that helps create alignment. The Product Backlog is the plan for future Sprints; it is a living plan, open to change and continually being evolved, as long as the product exists. Therefore, Product Backlog refinement is how Scrum Teams plan an upcoming Sprint, as well as future Sprints, which then impact the higher-level plans for business areas.

In our training classes, people often ask why Product Backlog refinement is not an event in Scrum. Because this activity is highly context dependent, it is an aspect of the Scrum Team's process—and is left to the team to determine the most effective practices and timing.

Many Scrum Teams struggle to find their rhythm with Product Backlog refinement. Common questions arise around how frequently to do it, how much time to spend on this activity, how much detail to get into, who is involved, and which practices to use. Again, this is something best determined by the Scrum Team and best learned by experimenting, inspecting, and adapting.

MINIMUM VIABLE PRODUCT BACKLOG REFINEMENT

The goal for Product Backlog refinement is minimal but sufficient. Product Backlog items (PBIs) have the attributes of a description, an order, an estimate, and value. This set of attributes reflects the minimum amount of information that an effective team should have before starting on a piece of work. Of course, all of these attributes are open to change as more information is learned.[6]

As PBIs become closer to being pulled into a Sprint, the Scrum Team will make some effort to break them down into smaller pieces and add details. PBIs will be deemed "ready" when the Development Team has a sufficient shared understanding of the value desired and believes the item to be small enough to get it to "Done" within a Sprint.

In Practice: Do You Need a Formal Definition of "Ready"?

We have seen the complementary practice of a formal definition of "Ready" used well, and we have seen it used poorly. Such a definition may be useful when a Scrum Team often runs into dependencies or gaps in understanding among the Development Team members that would be best handled during the refinement process, to avoid delays once a PBI is brought into a Sprint. Here are a few examples:

- Text requires review by the legal department
- Updated graphics are needed that align with branding/style guidelines
- Hardware or software needs provisioned and configured

---

6. ScrumGuides.org

> The way *not* to use a formal definition of "Ready" is to treat the PBIs like "locked down" requirements documents, in which all details must be written out and approved. This leads to an atmosphere of valuing "contract negotiation over collaboration."[7]
>
> Do not build an artificial barrier that prevents work from flowing to the Development Team or that means the Development Team cannot collaborate with the Product Owner or the relevant stakeholders. PBIs will continue to be refined even during the Sprint because more will be learned.

Scrum Teams should seek six benefits from Product Backlog refinement activities:

1. *Increased transparency.* The Product Backlog is the "single source of truth" for what is planned in the product. Adding details increases transparency to what you plan to deliver, as well as your progress.

2. *Clarification of value.* When you clarify the details around value, the outcomes you are trying to achieve with the PBI become clearer. This helps the Development Team build the right thing to meet the need. This can affect what is requested, the estimate, and the order as the Product Owner and the Development Team figure out what is actually needed.

3. *Breaking things into consumable pieces.* You want PBIs to be small enough that a Development Team can complete more than one in a Sprint. Having more than one PBI in a Sprint gives the team more flexibility to meet a Sprint Goal and deliver a "Done" Increment.[8]

4. *Reduction of dependencies.* Dependencies often turn into impediments. While you may not be able to avoid them all, try to reduce them where possible. At the very least, you want the dependencies to be transparent.

5. *Forecasting.* A refined Product Backlog combined with historical information about the Scrum Team's ability to deliver a working product helps you forecast. Forecasting for some products needs to stretch several

---

7. This is the opposite of valuing customer collaboration over contract negotiation, one of the core values in the Manifesto for Agile Software Development.

8. For more information on how to split user stories into smaller PBIs, see https://agileforall.com/patterns-for-splitting-user-stories/.

Sprints into the future to help communicate release expectations to stakeholders. For other products, forecasting beyond the current Sprint is unnecessary. Most products fall between these two extremes.

6. *Incorporation of learning.* Empiricism is about incorporating the learning you gain as you build the product, as you better understand how to realize product value, and as you see changes happening in your environment.[9]

With experience, you will find how much refinement is right for you to make planning easier while minimizing potential waste created by spending too much time refining.

ESTIMATION

The purpose of an estimate is to help a Development Team forecast what can be developed in a Sprint and to help a Product Owner manage a Product Backlog, specifically by determining whether an item has enough assumed value to warrant the investment in doing it (i.e., ROI). When we start to think about the bigger picture of forecasting and planning beyond a Sprint, estimates can help with this effort as well.

An estimate is really just a "guess" you make based on the best information you have about the size, effort, and complexity of a PBI. Because it is just a guess, you should assume every estimate is wrong; you should not expect estimates to accurately predict the future when you are doing complex work. When people are expected to be accurate in their estimates (either by a direct incentive or by an implicit measure of performance), this often leads to "gaming of the numbers." This then potentially leads to inflated estimates (which means they are no longer transparent and no longer serve their purpose) or cutting corners to meet an estimate (which means the Increment is no longer transparent and there is no way to deliver value).

Scrum does not prescribe how to estimate, but it does state that the Development Team owns the estimates because they are the ones doing the

---

9. Learn more about these benefits in this blog post: https://www.scrum.org/resources/blog/art-product-backlog-refinement.

work. These team members are accountable for creating the "Done" Increment, and they own the Sprint Backlog, which means they decide how much work to pull into the Sprint. This is an important aspect of self-organization.

You can approach estimation in two different ways: You can estimate the effort necessary, represented by hours or working days, or you can do relative estimation, which means you compare a chunk of work to something else based on an understood reference point. Empiricism and an agile mindset bias teams toward relative estimation because that approach helps teams incorporate complexity and unknowns, is based on experience with known work, and minimizes the amount of time spent on estimation (i.e., potential waste). The techniques you use are not as important as how you are using them and which benefits the Scrum Team is gaining.

In Practice: Leverage Teamwork, Empiricism, and an Agile Mindset with Relative Estimation Techniques

We have experienced success by helping teams select a relative estimation technique and leverage the power of group estimation. Here is a brief description of five commonly used relative estimation techniques:

- *Story points:* PBIs are estimated using a series of numbers, often the Fibonacci sequence (1, 2, 3, 5, 8, 13, etc.), to assign points to an item based on size and complexity.

- *T-shirt sizes:* PBIs are estimated using T-shirt sizes such as X-Small, Small, Medium, Large, and X-Large.

- *Animals, fruits, etc.:* PBIs are estimated using a physical object to represent relative size. For example, a watermelon is bigger than a cantaloupe, which is bigger than a grapefruit, which is bigger than a lime, etc.

- *"Same-size" items:* PBIs are sliced and split to have them all be roughly the same size.

- *"Right-size" items:* Essentially, this is breaking things down small enough that at least one item can be delivered in a Sprint.

Research indicates that **group estimation** is more accurate than individual estimation. It requires that groups have diversity and independence and that authority is decentralized within the group. The best decisions come from having productive conflict such that all perspectives are heard and the group can come to consensus.[10]

Consider engaging the entire Scrum Team in estimation. All the Development Team members can offer unique perspectives based on their own experiences, knowledge, and skills. Although the Product Owner does not estimate the work, this person's participation helps clarify the purpose and desired value of the PBIs. The Scrum Master helps ensure the team is collaborating well and doesn't fall into antipatterns involved with estimation (e.g., anchoring, analysis paralysis).[11]

BREAKING PBIS DOWN TO FOCUS ON VALUABLE OUTCOMES

Teams often struggle with breaking down big features and functions into valuable PBIs that are small enough to get to "Done" in a Sprint. We often see the focus being more on "small enough" while losing sight of "valuable."

Product Backlog refinement brings transparency to both the Scrum Team and the stakeholders about what the team is planning to build to deliver value. The Scrum Team needs to have a shared understanding of the desired outcomes to build the right thing. The Product Owner gains more flexibility and understanding of how to order the Product Backlog to optimize value. Stakeholders gain more transparency into how the work the Scrum Team is doing at the Sprint level connects to the larger things the business wants to achieve for the product.

Consider collaborative visualization techniques such as User Story Mapping, which enable the Scrum Team and stakeholders to see both the big picture

---

10. *Wisdom of Crowds* by James Surowiecki (Anchor, 2005).
11. To learn more about estimation techniques, see the book *Agile Estimating and Planning* by Mike Cohn (Prentice Hall, 2005).

and possible ways to break it down, while not losing sight of the user outcomes and value.[12]

No matter which techniques you employ, be sure that your Scrum Team and stakeholders are getting the six benefits described previously from breaking down the PBIs. Know why you are using a technique, and regularly inspect on how well that technique is meeting your needs. Adapt techniques to work better for you.

PLANNING A SPRINT

In the process of planning a Sprint, the Scrum Team should answer these three questions:

- What is the right work to focus on this Sprint, and how well do we understand it?
- How much can we get "Done" in a Sprint?
- How much time do we need to spend on improving how we work this Sprint?[13]

We've already talked about the first question. We will focus on the other two questions here.

How Much Can You Get "Done" in a Sprint?

As they plan the Sprint, the members of a Development Team select items from the Product Backlog that they believe they can complete in the current Sprint to achieve the Sprint Goal. How much they can get "Done" depends on their experience working as a team, the effectiveness of their team's processes, and their demonstrated ability to do similar work.

---

12. To learn more about user story mapping, see the book *User Story Mapping* by Jeff Patton (O'Reilly Media, 2014).

13. Refresh your knowledge of the basics of the Sprint Planning event (purpose, inputs, outputs) here: https://www.scrum.org/resources/what-is-sprint-planning.

As Scrum Teams grow their team identity and clarify and improve upon their ability to build quality releasable Increments, they will get better at having an intuitive sense of how much product they can build in a given period of time. The Sprint helps provide a cadence, or rhythm, for this intuitive sense to grow over time.

Here are some common challenges that will make it difficult to develop that intuitive sense:

- Frequent change in team composition
- Lack of collaboration
- Frequent change in the length of Sprints
- Team members being split across other teams or pulled away
- Frequent interruptions that lead to context switching[14]
- Partially done work at the end of a Sprint

To overcome these challenges, strive to create more stability and greater focus. Can team composition change? Yes, but it should be done intentionally and in a way that provides the team with sufficient control. Can a Sprint length change? Yes, but it should be done intentionally. Can there be interruptions? Yes, but they should be for good reasons and be done in ways that minimize their negative impacts.

And the reality is that the longer a Sprint is, the harder it is to plan. Longer Sprints have more complexity and more unknowns. If we asked you to plan out every single thing you can accomplish in the next month, that challenge would likely feel very overwhelming. But if we asked you to plan out your accomplishments for the next week, that would probably seem much easier.[15]

---

14. After each interruption, it can take more than 20 minutes for a person to get back to where he or she left off; see https://www.washingtonpost.com/news/inspired-life/wp/2015/06/01/interruptions-at-work-can-cost-you-up-to-6-hours-a-day-heres-how-to-avoid-them/?noredirect=on&utm_term=.8f892c76b64d.
15. To learn an approach to facilitating a Sprint Planning event, watch this short video: https://www.scrum.org/resources/effective-sprint-planning.

In Practice: How Long Should the Sprint Be?

"A Sprint should be as short as possible and no shorter." —Ken Schwaber

Scrum tells us a Sprint must be one month or less. But how do you know what is right for you? Two factors determine Sprint length:

1. How quickly does the business need to change direction?

2. How quickly can the Development Team create a "Done" Increment?

The first question is about enabling the business to take advantage of opportunities, respond to changes in the market, and manage its investment risk. A Product Owner will also need to consider how frequently feedback and new information will be collected and incorporated given the inspection and adaptation cycle of a Sprint.

Often we see that Scrum Teams focus on the second question. But if the answer to the second question is limiting business agility, then the Development Team should consider how to improve the necessary processes, tools, and capabilities to meet the business need. As an example, if the marketplace changes so frequently that there will never be four weeks of stable work available, then a four-week Sprint does not meet the business need.

Once a Sprint starts, its length doesn't change. However, a Scrum Team can choose to change the length of a Sprint for continuous improvement (usually determined in a Sprint Retrospective as the current Sprint concludes), with the decision applying to all future Sprints. The point is to allow the team to settle into a rhythm.

It may be helpful to align Sprint length with an "organizational heartbeat." For example, when multiple Scrum Teams are working on one product or product suite, coordinating work and resolving dependencies through aligning cadence becomes more important.

In Practice: Forecasting a Sprint with Empirical Data

Velocity is a complementary practice that provides an indication of the average amount of Product Backlog turned into a "Done" Increment during a Sprint by a Development Team. It is tracked by the Development Team for use within the Scrum Team. When historical data is gathered over time, a Scrum Team gains an understanding of the rate at which work has been completed and then can use this knowledge to forecast future work (i.e., to select PBIs for the Sprint Backlog).

However, velocity can easily be misused. It is crucial to understand what velocity is *not*:

- A performance measure of the Development Team
- A promise of what will be delivered in the future
- A way to compare Scrum Teams or Development Teams
- A way to compare individuals on a Development Team
- An indication of "how hard" a Development Team is working

In Practice: Probabilistic Forecasting

Probabilistic forecasting is an approach by which historical process data is used in conjunction with a statistical sampling method (e.g., Monte Carlo simulation) to make a prediction about when an item or items will be completed. This technique is popular with flow-based processes, as flow metrics are particularly conducive to statistical analysis.

The output of such a forecast is a statement about the future, cast in probabilistic terms within some agreed confidence level. In other words, a probabilistic forecast includes a range of possible future outcomes as well as a confidence level of that range occurring. For example, a team might use historical cycle-time data to offer an expectation that individual items will flow through their process in "8 days or less 85 percent of the time." Or they might use historical throughput data as input into a Monte Carlo simulation to forecast the chance of completing all items in the Product Backlog as "on or before October 1 with a 95 percent confidence."

The power of probabilistic forecasting lies in the fact that it embraces the intrinsic uncertainty associated with predicting the future. Whenever uncertainty is present, a probabilistic approach is warranted. Moreover, understanding the probabilities associated with certain outcomes is advantageous when assessing the risk that accompanies a given plan.[16]

---

16. For more details on probabilistic forecasting, see the book *When Will It Be Done* by Daniel Vacanti: https://leanpub.com/whenwillitbedone.

How Much Time Should You Spend on Improving This Sprint?

There is always pressure to deliver more value. Unfortunately, that often gets interpreted as "deliver more stuff." We often see that to deliver more value, Scrum Teams need to focus on improving how they work together, improving their tools, removing technical debt, and incorporating new learning.

In 2017, the Scrum Guide was updated to make explicit that the Sprint Backlog must include at least one high-priority process improvement identified in the previous Sprint Retrospective.[17] How much time is spent on continuous improvement is left up to the Scrum Team to decide. If a team is still struggling to create a "Done" Increment during every Sprint, the team members will likely need to spend more time on improving their practices, tools, and interactions. Of course, this means taking on less work right now, while acknowledging that this investment in improvement will create opportunities to increase the flow of value in the future.

How Far Ahead to Refine

A Product Owner ensures that there is a healthy Product Backlog of "just enough" refined work understood by the Development Team. The desire for prioritization is made clear through the order of the Product Backlog and an overall understanding of value and how it relates to business goals. The Development Team determines how much they can consume in a Sprint, and they learn to find the right balance over time. They can use empirical data—specifically, how much of the Product Backlog they have finished in previous Sprints—to forecast how much they might finish in future Sprints, but this forecast also takes into consideration how much change is expected in the menu and their appetite during the period being forecasted.

---

17. This has always been the expectation since the inception of Scrum, because inspection without adaptation is pointless.

You may also need to forecast at higher levels. Perhaps you need to forecast when a subset of PBIs is likely be delivered to achieve a business goal … and then the next business goal … and the next. Perhaps you need to forecast when a particular PBI in the Product Backlog is likely to be delivered.

PLANNING RELEASES

The purpose of planning is to communicate and manage expectations. We also plan so as to have something to measure progress against. As part of the rapid pace of modern society, people are seeking faster solutions to their concerns. The way to delight them is to either preempt or cultivate the desire for a feature, or be exceptionally responsive. This approach lies at the heart of Scrum—that is, in being able to release as quickly as necessary given the context of the product and the market in which it is used. A release is how you actually deliver value to users/customers.

The word "release" appears frequently in the Scrum Guide, yet Scrum does not prescribe release strategies or release planning. What Scrum does tell us is that as a part of the accountability to optimize value, it is the Product Owner's responsibility to decide when to release a "Done" Increment.

Some people ask, "Why isn't release planning a Scrum event?" Well, you don't have to release at all in a Sprint. In fact, you could go several Sprints before releasing. Or you could release multiple times in a Sprint, perhaps every time a PBI meets the definition of "Done." Netflix engineers release thousands of times per day because they are running lots of small experiments, the risk of any one of those changes causing a problem is very low, and the cost of backing out the change is also very low.[18] By contrast, a team that builds software for implanted medical devices will release very infrequently because the risk of causing harm if an error occurs is very high, and the cost of a re-release or product recall is exceptionally high. Each product will have an ideal release frequency that reflects its risk and cost of change.

---

18. For a brief introduction to modern release practices, see https://medium.com/data-ops/how-software-teams-accelerated-average-release-frequency-from-three-weeks-to-three-minutes-d2aaa9cca918.

How Large Should a Release Be?

The release strategy employed will depend on the type of product, the environment in which the product is used, and the capabilities of the Scrum Team. Therefore, the level of planning needed and the way to do the planning will be highly dependent on the release strategy. Release planning is best considered a part of the Scrum Team's empirical process, so that the team determines when and how best to do it to maximize benefits and reduce waste.

How Small Can a Release Be?

The smallest release you should consider is a *new or improved outcome* for a single *persona*. If you don't deliver at least that much to your customers, you will go through a lot of effort and your customers will not receive any benefit. If you deliver more than one new or improved outcome, you have prevented your customer from receiving the benefit of one of the outcomes earlier.

It may not be possible for you to release a single outcome at a time. You may have too much manual effort or complexity in your release process to make this possible. You may lack sufficient testing to ensure quality, or you may lack automation of key release activities. No matter how frequently you release, or how small the Increment is, removing these barriers will help you to improve the quality, cost, and frequency of your product releases.[19]

Summary

Plans are living artifacts: The activity of planning is what matters. Work on what you can control—creating the shared understanding, getting really good at delivering smaller pieces of value, and making sure you're always working on the next right thing. It will then be easier to adapt your plan when change inevitably happens.

---

19. For more information about release planning strategies, see *The Professional Product Owner* by Don McGreal and Ralph Jocham, also part of the *Professional Scrum Series* by Scrum.org, published by Pearson Addison-Wesley (2018).

The Product Backlog combined with empirical data is all you need to plan and forecast. It really is that simple. Over time, you will adjust your plan as you learn by doing the work and observing what is changing around you.

- The Product Backlog is the plan for future Sprints.
- The Sprint Backlog is the plan for the current Sprint.
- Product Backlog refinement is the planning activity.

Seek to maximize the value of planning activities while reducing waste. Accept that plans will evolve, and be vigilant about evolving plans as you learn. Enable transparency to progress so that you can set realistic expectations, and have open and honest conversations about the inherent complexity and unpredictability in product development.

CALL TO ACTION

Consider these questions with your team:

- Do planning activities feel light or heavy?
- How well do you collaborate as a team for planning and forecasting?
- How much change do you experience in the Product Backlog from Sprint to Sprint? How much Product Backlog does it make sense to have "Ready"?
- How well do the Scrum Team and stakeholders understand the value desired for individual PBIs?
- What benefits would be gained from releasing more frequently? What is holding you back from releasing more frequently?
- How do planning cycles in your organization enable empirical planning and alignment between the bigger picture business objectives and the work being done by the Scrum Team?
- What challenges are hurting the most right now? Identify one or two experiments to help improve the effectiveness of planning. For each experiment, be sure to identify the desired impacts and how you will measure them.

HELPING SCRUM TEAMS DEVELOP AND IMPROVE

Improving planning is important, but it is only one small aspect of the ways in which Scrum Teams can improve how they work together to deliver value. The need for these improvements is often revealed in the Sprint Retrospective, but it can also be revealed through feedback obtained in Sprint Reviews and through impediments surfaced throughout the Sprint.

Who helps the Scrum Team improve? The Scrum Master, most certainly, but not exclusively. In many cases, team members help each other to improve, and ideally the rest of the organization helps the team to improve. Leaders in the organization can play a big role in helping the team. But ultimately, the Scrum Team itself is responsible for improving itself and asking for help when needed.

USING THE SPRINT RETROSPECTIVE TO UNCOVER AREAS FOR IMPROVEMENT

When the Scrum Team fails to deliver a "Done" Product Increment, the focus in the Sprint Retrospective needs to be how the team can get to "Done" in the next Sprint. A team that is able to effectively self-organize should be able to step back and understand what happened to prevent them from getting to "Done," but the very fact that the team did not suggests that they may not be effective—at least, not yet.

Similarly, if customers or other stakeholders are unhappy with the value being delivered (this assumes, of course, the Scrum Team is getting to "Done"), that would also be a focus for a Sprint Retrospective. How effectively is the Product Owner working with the Development Team to create a shared understanding of value? How effectively is the Scrum Team working with stakeholders to better understand and deliver value?

The Scrum Master plays a critical role in how effective the Scrum Team is in diagnosing both problems and other impediments. The team may need help to push through self-created boundaries. We have seen teams impede their ability to deliver by assuming constraints and limitations on what they are allowed to do. The Scrum Master needs to clarify to the team what is in its scope to challenge, what is fixed, and what it should constantly and firmly push against.

In Practice: Use "Force Field" Analysis to Understand Motivation to Change

One way to discover the team's motivation to change is to do a simple force field analysis with your group. This process will outline the factors influencing the change.[1] After listing the factors that are affecting the proposed change, weight the factors based on their influence. Figure 6-1 describes the factors affecting a focus on "Done."

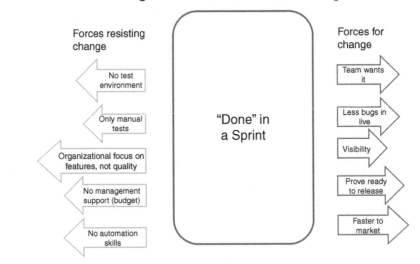

Figure 6-1 Force field analysis of "Done."

1. For more information about force field analysis, see www.mindtools.com.

> Making the process of working visible and bringing transparency to any impediment that slows the Scrum Team down is a good start. This may begin from the moment a feature is requested, and span all the way through implementation into the production environment. Teams and organizations tend to embrace change only when the cost of not changing exceeds the cost of changing. Force field analysis can help you have a discussion, as a team, about whether the change effort will be worth the cost.

In our experience, Scrum Teams struggle most with the Sprint Retrospective. Few people are comfortable with self-reflection and actively seeking areas where they need to improve. It's so much easier to focus on how to make the product more robust ("We should enhance that feature to support other business areas") or to complain about other teams ("It's always so difficult to work with them"). True self-reflection means being vulnerable, confronting limitations, and stretching to see other perspectives; most people find that very discomforting.

In Practice: Tips for Facilitating Sprint Retrospectives (and Any Other Collaborative Meeting)

Facilitation is an important skill when it comes to creating space for everyone's ideas and perspectives to be heard, as well as unlocking the creativity of a group's diverse experiences and areas of expertise, knowledge, and skills. The goal is to create productive conflict in a way that involves everyone in positive and creative collaboration, while getting to consensus-based decisions and clear outcomes.[2]

Here are some tips to improve your Sprint Retrospectives, which can be applied to any collaborative session:

- *Use silence.* Generally, silent facilitation techniques make space for people with personality preferences that may lead them to take time to think before speaking or to be hesitant to interrupt others during a lively conversation with strong voices. They can also be helpful when strong emotions are in play and you want to lower the level of conflict or, conversely, when artificial harmony is present and you need to create some conflict.

---

2. Facilitation is an entire profession, and we encourage you to explore the many resources available. For a deeper perspective on how to design and facilitate effective retrospectives, see *Agile Retrospectives: Making Good Teams Great* by Esther Derby and Diana Larsen (Pragmatic Bookshelf, 2006).

- *Use different group configurations.* Many challenges can arise with group discussions, especially as the size of the group increases. One or two people may dominate the conversation. While listening to others speak, people may form questions and new ideas but end up waiting until they see an opportunity to talk. At this point, their comments may not seem relevant or may even be forgotten. Furthermore, some people are more comfortable speaking one-on-one or in smaller groups.

- *Get people moving and taking action.* This immediately engages and involves everyone. People are less likely to get distracted or bored. For example, if people are switching partners or groups, they are physically moving. Another example is to have people make their conversations and results visible using flip charts.

- *Shake things up.* What we mean is to shock people's brains a bit, to challenge them to think differently and create some new perspectives. Changing up facilitation formats and techniques helps prevent people from just "going through the motions" or losing interest.

- *Come in with an agenda but be flexible.* Generally, you are seeking to (1) review transparent information to (2) generate new insights and then (3) decide on what actions will be taken for improvement. Have a plan for accomplishing each of those things, including the time expected to be spent on each. But be flexible and respond to the needs of the team while upholding the purpose of the event and the time-box.

IDENTIFYING AND REMOVING IMPEDIMENTS

For a Scrum Team to have a powerful Sprint Retrospective, its members must be able to identify impediments, ideally throughout the Sprint, that prevent them from creating a releasable Increment that meets the Sprint Goal. An **impediment** is anything that blocks or slows the Scrum Team's ability to deliver a valuable releasable product. The Development Team and Product Owner can and should resolve some impediments on their own (e.g., how they do their work to meet their accountability), perhaps with coaching and facilitation support from the Scrum Master. Impediments that Scrum Team members cannot resolve on their own are taken up by the Scrum Master.

By understanding the system that the team is working in as a whole, you will be able to identify what is impeding or holding the team back. Sometimes you can get more movement by releasing a brake than you can by pulling harder.

Scrum Teams maximize flow when they move items through the process as quickly as possible, without any risk to quality and customer satisfaction. Removing waste enables them to maximize flow—and by "waste," we mean anything that doesn't add value to a customer. To maximize flow you should look beyond just *blocking* impediments, by also focusing on things that slow the team down and prevent them from delivering the most value; don't wait until impediments become full-blown barriers.

Teams improve by creating more transparency into the things that may be slowing them down in their process so that they can identify the impediment and then figure out how best to tackle it. Scrum Boards are a common practice to visualize the progress of work. Visualizing the work helps the Development Team see when work is blocked or moving slowly, and there are many details to visualize beyond just using a Scrum Board.

In Practice: Create Transparency with a "Waste Snake"

Figure 6-2 visualizes waste in a team's work activities. You can create a snake-like chain of sticky notes, each summarizing something the team has to do that the team members consider to be wasteful. Prep the team by discussing sources of waste and what information to capture on each sticky note, such as the initials of the person, a short statement of the wasteful activity, the category of waste, and how much time was spent on the activity. This exercise provides a simple way for team members to capture the waste as they work during the Sprint. You can use it during the Sprint Retrospective to get a bigger picture of the trends and the costs and then discuss actions to reduce the wasteful activities.

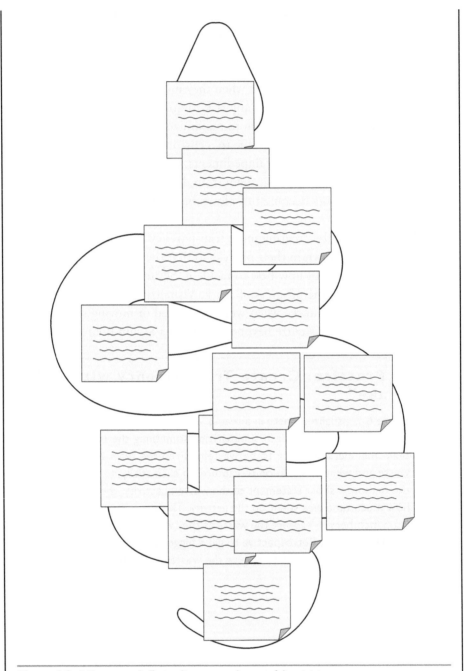

Figure 6-2 A "waste snake" visualizes a team's wasteful activities.

Common wasteful activities include the following:

- Manual regression testing
- Environments not available when needed, including crashes and restarts
- Starting work on a PBI and then discovering it has a dependency on another team and cannot be resolved during the Sprint
- Filling out requests for other teams to perform activities and encountering delays in their response (e.g., access to logs, changing a network setting, restarting a system)
- Filling out a security review form that has many irrelevant or unclear questions, which takes a lot of time and often requires additional follow-ups for clarification
- A team member being interrupted constantly and having to spend time reorienting himself or herself back to the work
- A poorly documented aspect of the system, which causes team members to have to relearn by asking other team members and researching every time they need to work in that area
- Detailing too much of the "how" for all PBIs during Sprint Planning and having to rework many of the tasks in the Sprint Backlog as the work unfolds

TRACKING IMPEDIMENTS AND QUANTIFYING IMPACTS

Given the many impediments teams face when doing complex work, it is likely that not all impediments will be immediately addressed when they are identified in a Sprint. Make this data visible and look for trends, indicating which impediments are within the Scrum Team's control, which are within the Scrum Team's influence, and which are external to the Scrum Team (see Figure 6-3).

ID	Impediment	Impact	Date Identified	Frequency	Action	Owner
1	Do not have lower environments that match production closely enough.	Deployment issues impacting customers (most significant March release).	Sprint 03	Every release	PO to secure funding to enhance environments and add this to PB. Dev Team will work directly with Infrastructure to design solution.	Product Owner
2	Dev Team does not have access to database.	Delays with troubleshooting during Sprint, usually takes between 2 hours and up to a day.	Sprint 03	Average 3 times per Sprint	Will require an exception to the existing policy. SM to work with IT management to get details on the exception process.	Scrum Master
3	Dev Team getting pulled into meetings frequently to consult on integrations for future projects.	Work interruption/context switching, takes time away from working on current Sprint Goal.	Sprint 04	Sprint 03 - 10 hrs Sprint 04 - 14 hrs	TBD - How can we support other teams in the organization while maintaining appropriate focus on delivery?	TBD

Figure 6-3 Impediments chart example.

Here are some useful questions to gain a better understanding of the impacts:

- How much time are we spending dealing with an impediment?
- How frequently is this impediment occurring?
- How is the impact affecting quality? Is the number of defects discovered in production increasing or decreasing? What is the cost of fixing a defect in production versus fixing a defect found during development?
- How is the impediment affecting morale? Are people leaving because they are unhappy with the impediment? What is the cost of hiring someone new?

In Practice: Tracking Interruptions Over Time

Tracking interruptions as an explicit type of impediment helps to quantify the impact of loss of focus. It doesn't matter whether the team actually takes on the work; merely being interrupted causes team members to lose productive time while they seek to regain their concentration.

You can track this data in a very simple way. Draw a timeline in the team's room, with a space for each day of the Sprint. Then, whenever a Development Team member is interrupted with unplanned work not aligned to the current Sprint Goal, he or she can write what it was on a sticky note and place it on the timeline. It can be helpful to include the source of the request (e.g., another team, a manager, a user, production issue) and how much time was spent dealing with the interruption. This information can be reviewed in the Sprint Retrospective to help the Scrum Team inspect the impacts and help guide actionable commitments for improvement.

Examples of interruptions include the following events:

- Bugs, incidents, and production support questions
- Additional work assigned by a team's manager
- Requests for time with team subject-matter experts
- A "drive-by" from a stakeholder wanting to chat with a developer about a new idea
- Requests to estimate potential future work
- Getting kicked out of a conference room and having to move somewhere else to finish a collaboration session

Not all interruptions are bad, but increasing transparency into interruptions and their impacts helps the Scrum Team determine how to make the necessary interruptions more valuable and effective (e.g., schedule specific time for a certain type of activity) and how to eliminate or reduce the unnecessary interruptions.

TACKLING IMPEDIMENTS

Once you have transparency into impediments, you can build a case for investing time and money to resolve those impediments. Of course, you will need to prioritize what you take on first. Some questions can help you decide where to start:

1. What goal do we need to achieve? What is our desired outcome?

2. What will happen if we don't tackle this impediment now?

3. What would we do if we could do anything we want to solve this problem? What constraints limit our options? Are they really constraints, or are we making assumptions?

4. If an organizational policy or standard stands in our way, can we change it, suspend it, or work around it?

5. How will we know if we are improving the situation (related to our desired outcome)?

6. Whose knowledge, support, or influence do we need?

In Practice: Engaging Stakeholders to Remove Impediments

Don't be afraid to talk about some impediments in the Sprint Review. Some things are best handled within the Scrum Team during the Sprint Retrospective, but it may make sense to bring up organizational impediments or impediments that require investing in the Scrum Team in the context of the Sprint Review. A wide range of stakeholders are in attendance in those sessions, and they may have influence (or money) to assist with these impediments.

Scrum Masters are responsible for resolving impediments that the Scrum Team cannot resolve themselves. However, Scrum Masters should not feel they have to tackle these impediments on their own. Often, managers or other roles in the organization (e.g., project managers) have great knowledge of how the organization works and its history. Scrum Masters should seek to partner with people who can provide additional knowledge, insights, and influence to tackle organizational impediments. And sometimes a Scrum Master just needs to ask for someone to provide a little "cover."

In Practice: Don't Focus on Velocity

Many organizations seek agility to improve their "speed," which causes them to focus on improving velocity. Velocity is empirical evidence, a historical fact, that is useful only for the Scrum Team. Usually, when a manager wants to know how to "improve velocity," the person is really just asking, "How can we deliver greater value more frequently?" In our experience, the best thing to do is to focus on removing impediments and waste. Focusing on velocity can lead to cutting corners and reducing quality in the rush to "go faster." Focusing on removing waste and impediments, by contrast, actually increases quality and leaves more time for doing the job right in the first place, while at the same time improving delivery speed.

Velocity going higher or lower is meaningless without context. A Development Team may deliver greater value, more frequently, and with higher quality, without any change in its velocity by simply taking into account improvements in its ways of working when it estimates.

Focus on removing the things that are holding the Scrum Team back, instead. Let the Scrum Team own its "delivery metrics," and focus stakeholders on "value metrics."[3]

GROWING INDIVIDUAL AND TEAM CAPABILITIES

Scrum itself doesn't solve problems. Instead, people are the ones who have to solve the problems that the Scrum Framework exposes, creating high-value solutions with an agile mindset and teamwork. To do this, they need to be given the space and the support to grow their capabilities. Every member of a Scrum Team must hone his or her "technical craft."

By "technical craft," we don't mean just engineering or software development skills. Product Owners need to develop a broad range of product management skills, while Development Teams need a wide range of skills related to creating a releasable Increment of value. Everyone needs to inspect and adapt their skills, knowledge, and capabilities and look at where the Scrum Team needs to grow so that it can meet new challenges and business needs.

---

3. https://www.scrum.org/resources/blog/why-focus-velocity-inhibits-agility

MAKE TIME FOR CONTINUOUS LEARNING AND GROWTH

Product development is complex and constantly evolving. New technologies and new insights into customer problems create new opportunities. Scrum Teams don't just inspect and adapt their product based on new information; they also inspect and adapt their own skills based on their experiences and the challenges they foresee. Learning and development is an aspect of self-organization. It is best to let the individuals and team own it, with support and guidance.

Continuous learning can take many shapes and forms: spending time on independent study, using online forums, attending webinars and meetups, attending or speaking at conferences, and reading books, articles, and case studies. It may include online training or an in-depth classroom experience, possibly including earning certifications (i.e., validation of learning). It may include having coaches or mentors, whether through formal or informal relationships. It may simply be people collaborating on their work, learning from each other, and getting real-time input and feedback.

In Practice: Pairing Beyond Programming

You may have heard of pair programming, in which two development team members collaborate on the same programming activity. They work together at one workstation. One person, deemed the "driver," writes code; the other, known as the "observer," reviews each line of code as it is written. The partners switch roles frequently. Throughout this process, they assist each other's work, discuss the design decisions, and provide immediate code review feedback.

You can extend this idea of pairing to create even more opportunities and benefits for a team. For example, two Development Team members might work as a pair, where one has stronger programming skills and the other has stronger testing skills (or database skills, or some other skills). Two Development Team members might also pair up for testing activities (e.g., designing tests, writing tests, executing tests).

Pairing helps provide two sets of eyes, brings different perspectives from people with varied skills and experiences, and grows the overall knowledge and skills of the team. Qualitative evidence suggests that pairing results in better design, fewer mistakes, an increase in learning, faster problem solving, and more accountability.[4]

---

4. This conference talk by Professional Scrum Trainer Pradeepa Narayanaswamy illuminates the benefits of pair testing as a means to grow skills: https://www.youtube.com/watch?v=DJBKWUjw01w.

> ## In Practice: Respect People by Training Everyone Who Needs It
>
> We often encounter situations where organizations have sent Scrum Masters to Professional Scrum training but did not send the rest of the Scrum Team. The organization expected the Scrum Master to be able to give everyone a mini-training session after attending class.
>
> This situation can have several negative impacts. First, Scrum Team members may feel that the organization doesn't respect them or the work they do enough to invest in their learning. Second, Scrum Team members often don't have a solid understanding of the Scrum Framework and the intent of Scrum when they start their Sprints because they didn't get the full experience from a professional trainer. This does not set people up for success.

LEVERAGE KNOWLEDGE AND EXPERIENCE IN THE ORGANIZATION

Whether it's Scrum, facilitation, Java, data analytics, user experience, or any other area, there is likely a wide array of knowledge and experience just waiting to be tapped into within an organization. Generally, people are eager to share and to support others. Teaching and mentoring others also help people hone their craft, as well as provide a greater sense of purpose.

> ## In Practice: Communities of Practice Enable Sharing and Improvement
>
> A Community of Practice (CoP) is a group of people with a common interest. They share their experiences with each other and have a common desire to improve. In addition to supporting the growth of the participants, a CoP can graduate to helping reveal organizational impediments and guiding the organization.
>
> A CoP is quite open in terms of what it looks like and how events and activities are facilitated. Its activities may include community presentations, presenters from outside the community, Lean Coffee, problem-solving sessions, workshops, and social events.

In terms of structure, CoPs may form based on a variety of factors: roles (e.g., Scrum Master), disciplines (e.g., Product Management, Testing), skills (e.g., Java, Architecture), or anything else your heart desires. It's okay if there is overlap; people may want to join multiple CoPs.

Here are some tips for creating effective CoPs:

- Managers need to support communities by providing meeting spaces (physical, virtual, or both), time for people to participate in and contribute to their communities, and funding to support community activities.

- Let people join communities voluntarily; coercing membership usually dilutes the benefits of the CoP.

- Let people self-organize. CoP members should define how it will work, how it will evolve, and who will run the CoP activities.

- Pick a good location for events, one that enables the collaboration you are seeking to create. It helps to periodically meet in person, but also provide virtual ways of meeting when physical meetings are not possible.[5]

BEING AN ACCOUNTABLE SCRUM MASTER

A Scrum Master is accountable for ensuring Scrum is understood and enacted, thereby helping Scrum Teams and the organization to maximize the benefits of Scrum. Often this gets interpreted as simply making sure the Scrum Team is following the "rules" of the Scrum Framework and removing organizational impediments that are perhaps getting in the way of the Scrum Team following that framework. While that is true, the role of Scrum Master is so much bigger than that.

The Scrum Guide describes the Scrum Master as a servant-leader. With this style of leadership, a Scrum Master's success is measured by the growth and success of others. This happens through a Scrum Master's ability to influence individuals and teams to take greater responsibility for their actions and outcomes, inspiring people to higher greatness.

---

5. Watch this short video by Professional Scrum Trainers Stacy Martin and Ty Crockett on their experiences with how to start CoPs, fund CoPs, get greater participation, and much more: https://www.scrum.org/resources/overview-communities-practice.

While a Scrum Master does have authority over the Scrum process and may need to reinforce the basic rules of the framework with new teams, his or her intention of helping others improve fosters trust and inspires team members to follow by choice, not simply because of force. An effective Scrum Master exhibits the following qualities:

- *Leads by example.* The Scrum Master embodies the Scrum values and collaborative teamwork. She is open to change and trusts in empiricism to deal with ambiguity and unpredictability. By modeling this positive mindset and adaptive approach, she shows the way for others.

- *Enables and empowers others.* The Scrum Master doesn't solve people's problems but instead seeks to reveal opportunities for improvement through transparent information and open discussion. She knows that she doesn't have the "best answers" and values the collective intelligence of the Scrum Team.

- *Creates an environment of safety and is comfortable with failure.* When people are learning and doing complex work, they need to feel safe entering into conflict, challenging each other, and trying new things.

- *Listens first and learns to "read the room."* The Scrum Master seeks to facilitate consensus, ensuring people feel heard and are open to hearing other perspectives.

- *Cares deeply for people and is also willing to challenge when they are capable of more.* The Scrum Master assumes positive intent and doesn't judge people. She meets people where they are and helps them find their next step, inspiring them to hold themselves to even higher standards.

- *Operates with integrity and stays calm under pressure.* The Scrum Master's leadership provides consistency and stability for others to hold onto when they are feeling stressed and overwhelmed by the uncertainty around them.

- *Shows low tolerance for organizational impediments.* The Scrum Master is willing to speak truth to power, challenging the status quo and advocating for the team.

To whom is the Scrum Master accountable? Both the Scrum Team and, ultimately, the organization. The Scrum Master serves the Scrum Team in maximizing the benefits of Scrum. The Scrum Team serves the organization in delivering valuable products. However, there are many paradoxes a Scrum Master must navigate to be successful.

MEASURING THE SUCCESS OF A SCRUM MASTER

The success of a Scrum Master is based on the success of the Scrum Team. However, a Scrum Master must not be short-sighted and take actions that will undermine the longer-term success of a Scrum Team. Similar to how you want to analyze the trends of multiple types of data to understand product value, so you need multiple types of data and an examination of the trends to determine how well a Scrum Master is doing. Here are some questions to consider:

- Is the Scrum Team reliably creating a releasable Increment during every Sprint?
- Is the value of the Increment acceptable? Is it improving?
- Is quality of the Increment acceptable? Is it improving?
- Do team members enjoy their work, and are they continuously learning and growing? Or does the team seem to be stagnating and experiencing declining morale?
- Is the Scrum Team committed to continuously improving every Sprint?
- Do the Scrum Team members have a solid understanding of the Scrum Framework, and do they apply it consistently and purposefully? Or are they just "following the rules" because the Scrum Master tells them to?

A Scrum Master's success can be measured on a continuum, as depicted in Figure 6-4. On this continuum, trends (getting better/getting worse) are more important than point-in-time measures.

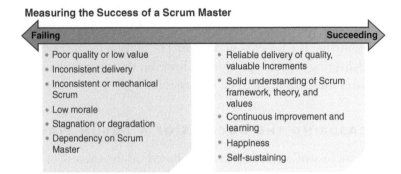

Figure 6-4 Success is demonstrated through the growth and success of others across multiple areas.

In Practice: Signs That a Scrum Master May Be Sacrificing Long-Term Success

Scrum Masters are often under pressure to "show improvement quickly." This challenging environment can lead to some behaviors that actually undermine the success of a Scrum Team:

- The Scrum Master facilitates the Daily Scrum or updates the Scrum Board to help "keep everything on track." A self-organizing team is capable of managing their own progress and updating their own plan. Early on, a Scrum Master may need to teach facilitation techniques and ask questions to help create focus and ensure consensus. Over time, however, the Scrum Master's direct involvement should increasingly diminish. In fact, if things go "off track," that failure may be the most powerful learning experience for the Scrum Team.

- The Scrum Master becomes a go-between when conflict arises between team members. People are better served when they learn to resolve their own conflicts directly with each other.

- When a Scrum Master is out of the office, the Scrum Team skips Scrum events. This can indicate either a lack of understanding of the purpose (i.e., not yet embracing empiricism) or a lack of skills (e.g., nobody feels comfortable facilitating a Sprint Retrospective).

Each of these behaviors demonstrates a dependency on the Scrum Master. In reality, Scrum Masters should aim to work themselves out of a job. While that will never actually happen, because teams will always face new challenges and have opportunities to improve, the Scrum Master should always seek better ways for the Scrum Team to be more self-supporting.

A Scrum Master is accountable to the organization, yet will often be in the position of challenging the organization when it stands in the way of the Scrum Team's success. The Scrum Master must show both courage and compassion to directly challenge people in leadership positions; learning how to deliver a difficult message with respect is crucial. Approaching people with openness and curiosity helps. In all that they do, Scrum Masters create shared understanding and involve people in developing collaborative solutions.

EFFECTIVE SCRUM MASTERS VARY THEIR APPROACH BASED ON CONTEXT

A Scrum Master relies on observation to understand where people are today and where they most need to grow. With experience, they develop an intuitive grasp of what to do in any given situation. They also continuously seek new information and recognize when it is time to change their approach (see Figure 6-5).

Figure 6-5 A Scrum Master must choose the best approach(es) based on context.

Scrum Masters will respond differently depending on the situation. Among their options are the following:

- *Uphold Scrum.* A new Scrum Team may not fully understand and embrace the empirical nature of the Scrum Framework. Team members may feel that they can skip an event, overrun a time-box, or lose sight of the accountability of their role without consequence. This may be because they are still struggling to build a strong team foundation, due to pressure from the organization to cut corners or because they have become complacent and started to let things slide. Upholding Scrum means guiding the Scrum Team back to the "why" behind the framework, reinforcing the benefits that being true to Scrum's principles provides.

- *Teach.* When a Scrum Team needs to improve its understanding of the foundations, core principles, and complementary practices of the Scrum Framework, a Scrum Master will need to help team members improve their understanding and apply that understanding to deliver value more effectively. They do this best by creating a space where people learn experientially through guided discovery.[6]

- *Point north.* In the context of Scrum, pointing north means creating and fostering an empirical culture of inspection and adaptation, with the intention to make better decisions by delivering value, gathering feedback, and changing course based on that feedback.

- *Coach.* When Scrum Masters coach, they embody the belief that the person or team has the capability of finding their own answers, and they help them find those answers. They focus on helping team members build an understanding of their situation and what they want to do next. This is usually done by asking questions to help them gain better understanding, identifying actions that they will take, and helping them be accountable for the actions.[7] Coaching helps people grow their ability to demonstrate

---

6. Tastycupcakes.org is a great crowdsourced repository of teaching activities for common agile concepts.

7. We encourage Scrum Masters and others who would like to improve their coaching skills to consider training from an organization accredited by the International Coach Federation (ICF). Organizations with which we have personal experiences with training include the Coach Training Institute (CTI) and Agile Coaching Institute (ACI).

responsibility, accountability, self-organization, and comfort with change and unpredictability.[8]

In Practice: Effective Scrum Masters (and Leaders) Coach Individuals for Better Team Results

In our experience, it is helpful to set aside regular time for coaching conversations with individuals on the Scrum Team (and even individuals outside the Scrum Team). Regular coaching conversations help people learn to understand themselves better. Coaching helps people tap into their purpose and clarify their values and vision. It also helps people understand their own preferences, motivations, and behaviors so that they can better manage their interactions with others.

Here are a few tips to get the most out of regular coaching conversations:

- *Try to get out of the regular work environment.* Perhaps take a walk around the building, go to a local coffee shop, or sit in a nearby park. A simple change in scenery, physical movement, or fresh air can bring about more perspective and creativity.

- *Don't always have an agenda.* While sometimes you may want to address specific observations or situations, let the person you are coaching drive the conversation. Coaching is about the other person, not about you. Simply start the conversation by asking, "What's on your mind?"[9]

- *Celebrate successes and growth.* While we do believe in continuous improvement, that can be sustained only by celebrating successes and growth along the way.

- *Make time to process observations and uncover learning.* If people are always in "action," they may not gain as many insights about themselves and their environment.

- *Facilitate.* Scrum Masters may facilitate Scrum events, additional working sessions, or even the flow of impromptu collaborations throughout the Sprint. Effective facilitation requires awareness (reading the room), constructive conflict, and maintaining a focus on shared goals and outcomes. Facilitating provides more structure for teams to self-organize and creates an environment in which team members can enter into productive conflict, explore multiple perspectives, commit to team decisions, and tap into their creativity.

---

8. For an example of how to combine coaching using the Scrum values, check out this blog post: https://www.agilesocks.com/4-ways-to-coach-with-the-scrum-values/.

9. "What's on your mind?" is one of the seven essential questions in the book *The Coaching Habit* by Michael Bungay Stanier (Box of Crayons Press, 2016). This is a great book that provides some easy-to-apply basics for coaching.

- *Take action.* In some circumstances, a Scrum Master will need to take action, sometimes decisively and immediately. In taking action, the Scrum Master acts as a protector of the team, its empirical process, and the interests of the broader organization. Taking action means that the Scrum Master must strike a delicate balance, guided by safety concerns. If the Scrum Master steps in too much or too frequently, they will damage the Scrum Team's ability to self-organize—but where the team's safety or integrity are threatened, the Scrum Master may have no alternative.

- *Actively do nothing.* Doing something for individuals when they could do it for themselves disempowers them. The heart of empiricism and a learning culture is experimentation, learning by doing. For the team members to learn, they need to act on their own. This is a conscious decision, and it is always in service of the learning and growth of others. The "active" part means you continue to actively observe while the team learns and explores. Then, based on what happens, you can continue this approach or choose something else.

In Practice: Where Scrum Master Intervention Is Appropriate

The Scrum Guide provides a simple example of an appropriate intervention by a Scrum Master: removing impediments, usually with input from the Scrum Team on the desired outcome that needs to be achieved. A Scrum Master in this situation will engage with others in the organization to help implement a solution, which often requires teaching, facilitation, and coaching.

When the safety of any person, the team, or the framework is in jeopardy, the Scrum Master must act. The extreme case is an instance of bullying or harassment. Not only is such conduct not aligned with the Scrum values and the core tenets of the framework, but it is also illegal. When something like this happens, the Scrum Master must act immediately to protect the team's safety.

A less extreme example is stepping in to actively manage a conflict that is escalating in an unhealthy way. Sometimes it is reasonable to let the team learn by exploring and doing; however, at other times, an intervention will help the team make a step change. This is particularly common with teams starting out, as they are not sure of how to work in this new way together. By more actively guiding the team, the Scrum Master can help improve the pace of learning.

SUMMARY

Scrum Teams need help and support to improve. They will likely identify many of the areas in which they need to improve in their Sprint Retrospectives, but they shouldn't overlook the power and immediacy of the Daily Scrum as a lens for improvements. Rapidly removing impediments as soon as Scrum Teams encounter them is perhaps the greatest thing you can do to help them.

Transparency helps everyone understand the things that are holding a team back, and keeping track of recurrent problems can help to make those challenges more visible. Visualizing various forms of waste and communicating them to people who can help remove them is a good habit to adopt.

Scrum Teams also need to invest in their own improvement and be given the space to do so by those outside the team. They need to account for personal and team development investments when planning Sprints, and they need to make their needs for development support transparent to people outside the team who may need to provide money, time, or the help of other people to develop their capabilities.

Scrum Masters play an important role both on their teams and beyond their teams. They help their teams learn and develop their skills, embrace empiricism and an agile mindset, challenge them to improve, and help them hone their capabilities. Being an effective Scrum Master requires a wide range of skills, along with the wisdom and expertise to know when and how to apply different techniques. Beyond the team, Scrum Masters help their teams by influencing the organization at large to help their Scrum Teams become more effective over time.

CALL TO ACTION

Consider these questions with your team:

- How much meaningful reflection happens in Sprint Retrospectives?
- In what ways could Sprint Retrospectives be more engaging, creative, and collaborative?

- What data do you have that could bring transparency into the frequency and the impacts of impediments?
- What actions have been taken to tackle impediments in the past few Sprints?
- What major impediments are being tolerated?
- In what areas do team members most need to and want to grow?
- In what areas is the Scrum Team improving, and how has the Scrum Master been influencing this growth?
- Is there anything a Scrum Master may need to stop doing?
- What do you need from leaders in the organization to support team improvement?
- What challenges are hurting the most right now? Identify one or two experiments to help improve. For each experiment, be sure to identify the desired impacts and how you will measure them.

Leveraging the Organization to Improve

As we explored in the previous chapter, the Scrum Master, managers, and even individuals within the Scrum Team help each other and the overall team to improve. In doing so, they will frequently need to leverage the organization's structure and culture to create the necessary conditions to help teams grow their capabilities and to improve the team's focus on frequently delivering value. The organization's structure and culture have a significant influence on a team's identity, its process, and how team members understand and measure product value. The challenge for everyone is to make the organization's influence a positive one, rather than one that impedes the growth of Scrum Teams.

Organizations Need to Evolve to Succeed

Every organization needs structure and constraints on how it works so that it can successfully run its business. The organization defines which products and services it offers to which customers, as well as the business models that make funding development and support activities possible. This structure also defines how employees, partners, and service providers work together to deliver products and services. The structure is often expressed in the processes and policies that the organization establishes and enforces.

Every organization also has a culture, a body of habits that bind people together and establish unwritten norms for behavior. This culture evolves from the sum of all human behavior within an organization and is influenced by the organizational structure and processes, including roles, goals, and incentives.

To help an organization get the most out of Scrum, you will typically need to evolve its culture, its processes, and possibly even its structure. To minimize harm to the organization and the Scrum Team, you need to do this intentionally; organizations and cultures have many inherent mechanisms, both explicit and implicit, to prevent accidental change. By introducing Scrum, you will inevitably introduce change, and the blow-back from unmanaged change is a frequent reason why Scrum Teams struggle, often without really understanding what is going on.

Scrum Teams can sometimes work for a while without tackling the structural and cultural challenges of the organization, but eventually they will start running into impediments that are outside of their control. When those impediments cannot be resolved, the Scrum Team will reach a plateau, and they will struggle to maintain progress.

In this chapter, we briefly explore the most common challenges that Scrum Teams encounter at the organizational level. We also describe how to pivot your mindset from "protecting the team from the organization" to "leveraging the organization to improve the Scrum Team's ability to deliver value."

DEVELOPING PEOPLE AND TEAMS

Organizations invest a lot of money in hiring and developing people, yet their actions can undermine their ability to retain and engage those same people over the course of their careers. Actively disengaged employees cost U.S. companies approximately a half a *trillion* dollars a year in lost value, to say nothing of the cost of the merely "not-engaged" employees. While it is no longer a reasonable expectation for people to stay at a company for their entire career, keeping employees purposefully engaged returns significant benefits.[1]

---

1. https://www.inc.com/ariana-ayu/the-enormous-cost-of-unhappy-employees.html

THE IMPACTS OF PERFORMANCE REVIEWS AND COMPENSATION

Traditional organizations focus primarily on individual performance. More realistically, in the modern world in which we live and work, nearly everything we do requires collaboration between many people to achieve the results we desire. Rewarding individuals for work achieved by a team is a short-sighted and outdated practice, and one that sends the wrong message about what is important. Often, teamwork and team outcomes are not even considered or are only a minor part of evaluation. Furthermore, many compensation systems can seem arbitrary and based on titles and status rather than effort, growth, and outcomes achieved. And do annual performance reviews even make sense anymore?[2]

In today's fast-paced world, high-performance teams are the value-creation engines of the organization. Organizations that want to create and nurture high-performance teams need to reward teamwork, not individual performance. They can do this in a variety of ways, including the following:

- Rewarding bonuses to teams, based on team results
- Letting teams decide how to distribute raises and bonuses among team members
- Heavily weighting contributions to the team when reviewing an individual's performance
- Providing people with frequent, meaningful, and actionable feedback
- Gathering feedback on an individual's performance from a wide range of people: team members, customers, and managers (sometimes called 360-degree feedback)[3]
- Considering intrinsic rewards that increase a person's or a team's sense of autonomy, mastery, and purpose[4]

---

2. https://www.forbes.com/sites/lizryan/2018/01/14/performance-reviews-are-pointless-and-insulting-so-why-do-they-still-exist/#1cf4ca8972d1; https://getlighthouse.com/blog/get-rid-of-the-performance-review/
3. https://www.thebalancecareers.com/360-degree-feedback-information-1917537
4. *Drive* by Dan Pink (Riverhead Books, 2011).

INDIVIDUAL CAREER PATHS

In our work with organizations, we are frequently asked about defining career paths. The role of Scrum Master is new to many organizations and is unlike any other role they have, so they are not sure how to define a career path. The same goes for Product Owner. Moreover, when managers begin to understand the self-organizing, cross-functional nature of Development Teams, they may realize that the way they have defined career paths can create conflicts.

Traditional organizations are often structured into skill-silos built around some area of specialized knowledge, each with its own career path. This structure made sense when work was indeed specialized and in a world in which people did not have to deeply collaborate to get work done. We have already shown the power of self-organizing, cross-functional teams when delivering complex products in a world that is more uncertain than certain. Siloed organizations with rigid roles cannot keep pace with the organization's changing needs; the best solution is to let the people closest to the product and customers decide which skills they need.

A career is—and really always has been—a story you tell yourself about how what you are doing now will lead to something else. It doesn't take a lot of self-reflection to realize that most of what you thought would happen didn't, but all sorts of wonderful things you couldn't have dreamed of happened instead. The other problem with the notion of a career is that innovation is creating new kinds of work all the time and killing off many other kinds of work. The job that you will be doing ten years from now either doesn't exist or will be so transformed that it won't resemble the way it's done today.

The agile world is, in many respects, a post-career world. In a complex environment characterized by constant change, the skills and knowledge needed to deliver value to customers will always be evolving. In place of career planning, organizations and individuals need to focus on building flexible problem-solving and critical-thinking skills. Self-organizing teams are a great vehicle for this type of growth because they let any team member volunteer to learn new skills when the team needs them.

At the same time, team members need some direction to help them make their own professional development decisions. Their organizations can help them in the following ways:

- Being transparent about which skills are needed in different parts of the organization, and where opportunities for developing those skills exist
- Helping them understand where they might need to grow their breadth of skills in addition to their depth of skills
- Connecting them with mentors who can provide career perspective and help them build a professional network
- Helping them grow their influence in the organization beyond their current team
- Supporting Communities of Practice to share and develop skills and experience
- Helping them to develop leadership skills in addition to technical or task-specific skills

SOURCING STRATEGIES AND TEAM IMPACTS

Organizations use sourcing strategies to achieve a variety of ends: lowering costs, increasing employment flexibility, and gaining quick access to scarce skills, to name a few. But these same strategies can affect the ability for teams to come together, to develop autonomy and identity, which will affect their ability to deliver value. Team members from different organizations can have different motivations and different levels of commitment to team goals. Contractors may not experience the same level of respect or trust as other team members. Team members at remote locations may not experience the same degree of transparency or inclusion. Sourcing strategies that treat people like exchangeable labor inputs are deeply damaging to creating the kind of accountable, transparent, self-organizing teams that are essential to success.

Sourcing strategies that focus on reducing labor rates without considering team effectiveness are short-sighted. Long wait times resulting from excessive hand-offs, effectiveness losses caused by excessive context-switching, and rework caused by ineffective communication can easily overwhelm the small savings accrued from in-house versus outsourced salary differences. Focus first on building high-performing teams, and then focus on removing impediments and other sources of waste, or you may simply find that your sourcing strategy achieves, as one manager we worked with lamented, "failure, 70 percent off."

In Practice: The Inherent Conflict in Outsourcing Production Support

Many organizations want to outsource their support work to save money, but outsourcing support work is often based on the flawed assumption that such work just requires commodity coding and bug fixing skills. Outsourcing support is often based on a project mindset that assumes changes to applications are infrequent and simply related to fixing defects.

When the application is part of a value stream that delivers value to customers, outsourcing support can be damaging in several ways. The assumption that applications should not change frequently is a bad one. In reality, applications and other processes in the value stream may change very frequently in response to changing markets or customer needs. Support processes that intentionally make this change difficult become an impediment to improving customer satisfaction and retention.

Likewise, outsourcing support deprives Scrum Teams of valuable information they need to understand how to make the application—their product—better. They never get experience with supporting the system, so they fail to invest in product capabilities that could improve the customer's experience by making the application more robust, scalable, or secure.

Outsourcing support forces developers and operations professionals into an inherently conflict-ridden relationship, prone to finger-pointing and animosity. Finally, it deprives support staff of valuable experience that can only be obtained by working on the product.

The reality is that support/operations is a complex task, and carving out support separately from development creates many problems and solves few.

If outsourcing is part of your strategy, consider these questions:

- Is this a transactional relationship or a longer-term partnership?
- How will the contractors get training and professional development? And will that be in alignment with that of the in-house employees they work with?

- Does the partner have an agile mindset and commitment to empiricism?
- How is the partnership assessed? What is the inspection and adaptation process for improvement?
- What risks does outsourcing pose to your business? What benefits does outsourcing provide to your business?

Outsourcing has its benefits, when used appropriately, but be aware of the costs (both direct and indirect) as well. Consider what the organization can do to reduce the risks of outsourcing. Observe outcomes and behaviors.

Distributed Teams

Similar to outsourcing, distributing team members can reduce the cohesion and effectiveness of a team. People working in different time zones will have less time to collaborate depending on how much their workdays overlap. People working at different sites will find that they may be less effective in their collaboration as compared to people who work side-by-side. They will find it more difficult to work together as a team. It is not impossible to make distributed teams work, but it is certainly much harder.

Team members from different cultures also sometimes struggle to communicate. Some cultures are more open to expressing differences of opinion, whereas other cultures are more deferential in the face of differing social status. These and other factors make transparency more challenging. Trust and time working together usually help team members reach greater levels of mutual understanding that makes transparency and collaboration more effective, but this shared mindset is harder to achieve when team members are remote. In any case, you will have to work more diligently to overcome the barriers created by distributed teams by taking the following steps:[5]

- Help the team to self-organize, rather than try to solve problems for them.
- Invest in the team's growth with on-site collaboration sessions (at least once a year; quarterly is more desirable). Include activities focused on

---

5. For other techniques, see https://techbeacon.com/app-dev-testing/distributed-agile-teams-8-hacks-make-them-work.

getting to know each other, establishing clear working agreements, aligning around product vision and understanding customers, and accomplishing shared goals together.

- Invest in communication and collaboration tools (e.g., video communication, interactive whiteboards).

GETTING COMFORTABLE WITH TRANSPARENCY

Throughout this book, we have discussed the importance of transparency when dealing with complexity, ambiguity, and unpredictability, as well as how it shows up in our everyday interactions. As Scrum Teams begin to embrace transparency and an empirical process, they often have to confront the harsh reality that the larger organization is not necessarily comfortable with transparency. Transparency sounds like a good idea until customer feedback shows that an important stakeholder's "must do" PBI wasn't something customers cared about or when it exposes that the most senior developer on the team needs to improve his code quality.

Transparency requires courage because it may challenge accepted hierarchies or dogmas. Transparency requires real leadership because the team needs to have safety and the psychological space to sometimes say things that are true but unpopular. More specifically, leaders need to ensure that the rest of the organization does not overtly or indirectly "punish" the messenger. As one of our former managers used to say, "Facts are friendly": It is always better to have more and better information to make better decisions. With better information, teams are able to more effectively inspect and adapt.

Many organizations and their executives have a bias toward positive people with a "we can do it" attitude. There is a lot of value to having a team that believes it can do anything. At the same time, there is a fine line between confidence and delusion. Transparency is an antidote to unrealistic expectations.

Psychological safety is essential to nurture effective teams.[6] Just as the individuals on a team need to feel trust with each other, the organization needs to demonstrate trust of the team. Trust means there is a willingness to:

- Have open and honest discussions.
- Share and explore dissenting opinions.
- Believe that everyone is doing their best with what they know at the time.

A Culture of Accountability, Not a Culture of Blame

When leaders say, "I need people to be more accountable," they sometimes really mean they want someone to blame when things go wrong. This creates a culture of fear that prevents people from trying new things, gathering feedback, and adapting. Agility cannot survive in an organization with a fear-based, blame-oriented culture. Accountability is different from blame. Yes, it does mean owning your decisions and the results of those decisions, but the ultimate goal is not to have someone to blame. Instead, accountability means being focused on the purpose and having the right intentions. It's about being transparent to how decisions were made, which enables learning and adaptation. It's about accepting complexity and unpredictability and about creating shorter feedback loops to reduce risk and learn sooner.

An organization with a culture of accountability lets people own the decisions they should own (i.e., no one trumps the Product Owner's decisions about what to build), demanding that they be empirical in their approach and supporting that with access to the people and information they need, and accepting that mistakes and surprising successes will happen along the way.

When organizations get comfortable with transparency and move from a culture of blame toward one of accountability, it requires leaders to let go of control—or rather, the illusion of control.

---

6. https://hbr.org/2017/08/high-performing-teams-need-psychological-safety-heres-how-to-create-it

LETTING GO OF (THE ILLUSION OF) CONTROL

Managers in traditional organizations live in a cultivated illusion that they are "in charge." Anyone who has filled a management role has come to realize how little control managers actually have, especially in cases where their organizations deliver complex products. There is simply no way for a manager to have all the knowledge and expertise needed to deliver great products. It really does take a cross-functional team that is capable of, and empowered to, make their own decisions. With accountability.

Until managers help teams to self-organize and take on that accountability, the team will never develop the skills, trust, transparency, commitment, focus, openness, courage, and respect that they need to deliver great results.[7] When a manager doesn't let go of the illusion of control to become a servant-leader, her teams will be mired in ineffectiveness and confusion.

THE REAL POWER OF THE IRON TRIANGLE

Recall the Iron Triangle from Chapter 5, "Improving Planning." As we noted in that chapter, the Iron Triangle often leads people to ignore outcomes as a measure of success. Something else that is important to understand about the triangle is that the three constraints of cost, schedule, and scope cannot all be fixed because we are dealing with complex work.

Somewhere along the way, this point gets lost in many organizations, which demand that scope, schedule, and cost all be estimated and guaranteed. The real power of the Iron Triangle emerges when organizations recognize they cannot fix all of these variables, and they instead have the right conversations, openly and honestly, about the constraints impacting the decision to pursue (or continue pursuing) a given opportunity.

- Can you deliver something of sufficient value quickly enough and for a cost that justifies the investment?

---

7. https://guntherverheyen.com/2013/05/03/theres-value-in-the-scrum-values/

- Do you have familiarity with the work to be done? How are you factoring that uncertainty into the decision to pursue the opportunity?
- How frequently can you validate that your answers to the preceding questions are still valid?

The old adage is you can fix only two sides of a triangle. Scrum make it quite easy to follow the "rules" of the Iron Triangle. If you think about a Sprint, it is a fixed amount of time and a fixed cost (assuming the people on the Scrum Team and their capacity are not changing). Thus, it becomes quite easy to fix time and cost with Scrum—and then you allow the scope to be flexible (see Figure 7-1).

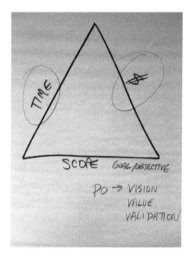

Figure 7-1 Iron Triangle with a product mindset. (Photo by Stephanie Ockerman.)

Although you might be concerned about scope being flexible, the reality is that we cannot predict what scope will lead to the desired outcome. Remember that Scrum gives us the Product Owner, who is accountable for optimizing value. The Product Owner creates alignment with a product vision, orders a Product Backlog, and defines and validates value. The Product Owner makes sure the Scrum Team is always working on the next right thing.

Of course, the Product Owner and stakeholders may not actually know what the right thing is to achieve desired outcomes. They may have ideas and hypotheses, but the complex nature of product development makes it challenging to know the right thing with absolute certainty. This goes back to the point of validating outcomes. The flexibility in scope represents the power of the Iron Triangle. And if you are releasing frequently to validate your assumptions and get meaningful feedback from the market or users, you can adapt your process to more closely align with the desired outcomes.

You might be wondering, "What if I want to fix two different sides of the Iron Triangle?" This is where we believe the traditional project management view creates a fallacy—specifically, because of complexity. Fixing time and scope is often desirable, but throwing more money at a complex problem without extending the schedule typically has the opposite effect. The options are to have everyone work overtime or to add more people to the team. The former burns people out, introducing quality issues and eventually reduced morale. The latter slows you down because you now have to deal with re-forming the team's identity and working through team process challenges with new team members.

The logical way to use the Iron Triangle is to fix time and money and let scope be flexible. Alternatively, you can fix scope and let the time and money be flexible, but only if you are absolutely sure that everything that you think you want is really needed by your customers.

FUNDING INITIATIVES

Many initiatives start with a goal or desired outcome in mind. Sometimes the organization has a hypothesis of what scope may help achieve the desired outcome. You might also want to understand an approximate cost to deliver that scope to achieve desired outcomes. This is when you do scope-based estimating. You can leverage the relative estimation techniques discussed in Chapter 5, but you would likely do this at a higher level.

SCOPE-BASED ESTIMATION

Scrum Team members that have been working together on a product can do relative estimation and compare this work to previous initiatives they have delivered. And if they do not have history working together, they will need to do just enough analysis to get an idea about the work, knowing they can create a revised estimate as they learn more during each Sprint.

At a high level, we recommend keeping estimates simple. A Product Owner conveys what is known about the initiative, including desired outcomes and the specific features or capabilities expected to achieve those desired outcomes. In turn, the Development Team estimates based on what is currently known. The smallest unit that can be budgeted for a Scrum Team is a Sprint. Therefore, it makes sense to create budgets in those units. Perhaps the Development Team will estimate a number of Sprints. Or perhaps the Development Team estimates the work as Small, Medium, or Large and establishes an understanding of what level of effort and complexity falls into those categories. The team will then have a rough forecast of how many Sprints it will take to complete the work— and the number of Sprints will provide the cost. Ultimately, it comes down to the number of Sprints. Figure 7-2 provides an example of a Scrum Team's estimation of high-level initiatives.

	High-Level Estimate (sprints)	Team Budget ($50K/Sprint)
Capability A	2	$100,000.00
Capability B	4	$200,000.00
Capability C	0.5	$25,000.00
Capability D	3	$150,000.00
Capability E	7	$350,000.00
Capability F	1	$50,000.00
Capability G	3	$150,000.00

Figure 7-2 Example of simple high-level budgeting.

Of course, you may have additional costs beyond the people in the Scrum Team, so you will need to estimate and add those costs into your budget. Remember to regularly inspect and adapt in case any of those nonlabor costs are expected to change as the work unfolds.

Even with scope-based budgeting, you still want scope to remain reasonably flexible so that the team can learn and adapt the Product Backlog closer toward the desired outcomes. This allows for adjusting the specific items in the release, while fixing the volume of work to be completed.

ITERATIVE AND INCREMENTAL BUDGETING

Scrum, done well, enables the business to iteratively and incrementally budget and fund a Scrum Team for a number of Sprints, trusting the Product Owner to make appropriate decisions about the order of the Product Backlog so as to optimize value. The "Done" Increments, along with new learnings about the work, value metrics, and customer feedback, are made transparent to stakeholders during every Sprint. (The Sprint Review is a great opportunity to discuss these lessons.) The Product Owner modifies the Product Backlog based on empirical evidence and collaboration with stakeholders and the rest of the Scrum Team. Keep in mind that the longer your Sprint, the more investment risk you carry.

At any point, a Product Owner or the organization can decide to stop funding additional Sprints. This may happen when the return on investment is no longer high enough to justify enhancements to the product. It may indicate that the organization has an opportunity to invest more in a different or new product, and the Scrum Team could be delivering more value working on something else. This is why having a "Done" Increment is essential, as it enables the business to respond to opportunities.

With products that have existed for a year or more and have consistently demonstrated value from continuously delivering enhancements, it may make sense to move to an iterative and incremental budgeting model. Perhaps it makes sense to fund a product and its Scrum Team(s) for an entire fiscal year. Consider the amount of overhead that you could save by not going through separate budgeting processes and maintaining separate budgets for each initiative impacting the product that year.

This type of budgeting aligns with ideas popularized by the *Beyond Budgeting* movement.[8] It argues that traditional budgeting processes rarely provide the value given the effort spent and often work against the organization becoming sustainable and adaptive. It makes a case that organizations should replace their centrally controlled, predetermined goals with self-regulating, relative benchmarks and transfer the decision-making authority to employees at the front lines.

Three factors affect planning and forecasting for longer time horizons:

1. Do you already have funding?
2. Do you have history (i.e., empirical data) to help you plan?
3. What is the level of trust in the organization?

In Practice: Evolving How You Plan and Fund a Product as You Grow Trust and Learn by Working as a Team

An existing Scrum Team has been working on a product for three months, so team members have history together with a known type of work. From this history, they have an intuitive understanding of approximately how big and complex work items are. Because they have been consistently delivering "Done" Increments and have been transparent with stakeholders about progress and how decisions about value are being made and validated, they have built up trust. If this product is already funded for another few months, it is likely that the team's Product Backlog is detailed for the next couple of Sprints. The Product Owner ensures the work at the top of the Product Backlog is the work that will best optimize value for the organization.

Next, consider a business leader who wants to build a new product and form a new Scrum Team to do it. The business leader needs to justify that the product offers a reasonable ROI, so enough planning must be done to get a high-level idea of the cost to achieve the initial product goals. If this organization has a culture of trust, an agile mindset, and experience with effective Scrum, a Scrum Team will do just enough analysis to come up with a high-level initial plan. They will regularly inspect and adapt the overall product initiative based on how the plan changes and as history is built with the new Scrum Team. The Product Owner will verify assumptions about ROI as the product is built. Additional funding can be requested if it makes sense to continue investing in enhancing the product.

---

8. For more information about *Beyond Budgeting*, see https://bbrt.org/the-beyond-budgeting-principles/.

> Now consider an example in which there is distrust within the organization. More up-front planning is often done because of a mistaken belief that this kind of planning will create certainty. A Scrum Team may spend weeks or even months detailing a Product Backlog, which costs money and delays delivery of value. And in our experience, once the work begins, the plan often changes as a result of feedback from a working product. The team will likely experience a lot of waste, in the form of throwing away earlier detailed analyses and changing details in the Product Backlog.
>
> With Scrum, you're going for "just right." That is, you want planning to be minimal but sufficient.

"BEING AGILE" IS NOT THE GOAL

A lot of organizations are pursuing an "agile transformation"; yours may be one of them. Wanting to be more agile is generally a good thing, except when "doing agile" becomes the goal. An agile mindset, agile frameworks (such as Scrum), and agile practices can help your organization achieve its goals, but the real goal is (or should be) improving the value the organization is delivering, whatever that means in this particular case.[9]

So what's the harm in focusing on "agile transformation"? Mainly, lack of focus, plus the risk of "zombie Scrum," in which people just go through the motions without really understanding what they are doing or why. If you're clear about what you want to achieve, stated in customer terms, you will be much more effective at making the trade-offs you will inevitably need to get there.[10]

---

9. For more on this topic, see https://www.scrum.org/resources/blog/scrum-transport-not-destination.

10. Scrum.org has created a measurement-based empirical improvement framework called Evidence-Based Management that provides ways of expressing goals and using measures to improve your ability to reach those goals. For more information, see https://www.scrum.org/resources/evidence-based-management.

> ## In Practice: Why Being "100 Percent Agile" Is a Bad Goal
>
> If "being agile" is not the goal, then being "100 percent agile" is even worse, as it pushes an agile approach on people and teams that may have no need for empiricism or innovation. If you want teams to deliver faster, break their work down into smaller increments and focus on removing their impediments. You need empiricism when you can't determine exactly what to build or how to build it. But if you know what you need and how to build it, then just do it. Don't hide behind some agile facade, thinking that it's a superior approach.
>
> Organizations that fall into the "if agile is a good thing, let's do it everywhere" trap have lost sight of what they are trying to achieve. They are also getting ahead of themselves. When agility works, it does so because empowered, self-organizing, highly professional teams are using agility to continuously inspect, adapt, and improve both their product and their way of working. It takes investments of time and money, plus the right people, to build these high-performing agile teams.

NAIL IT BEFORE YOU SCALE IT

Organizations sometimes get impatient and want to add more Scrum Teams to deliver more value. However, if the existing team is struggling to reliably deliver releasable Product Increments that customers and users find valuable, scaling is a bad idea. When you try to scale by adding more teams because you want them to deliver more, you are really just scaling the existing challenges, and you will amplify chaos and confusion.

Instead, focus on helping the Scrum Team be great. Often, removing organizational impediments, enabling team process improvements, and creating a better understanding of the business and customers will deliver the desired flow of value without the cost and additional complexities of multiple teams. If you do still think you need to scale to get where you want to go, you now have a solid foundation to build upon. Add one more team, and work through the new challenges to get back to great. Then add another team, and another, until you have satisfied your need for product delivery teams.

When scaling multiple Scrum Teams on the same product, do so intentionally, and leverage what brought you success in the first place. Empowered, self-organizing teams will determine when and how to scale, by continuously inspecting and adapting to improve both their product and their way of working.[11]

SUMMARY

The structure of an organization, its processes and policies, and its culture all have a strong, and sometimes overwhelming, influence on the teams that work within it. Learning to leverage the organization to promote a strong team identity, so as to help teams improve flow in their process and deliver greater product value, is essential to achieve long-term benefits from agile approaches like Scrum.

All organizations need to continuously evolve, whether or not they are using Scrum. How quickly they must evolve depends on where they are today, where they need to go, and which changes are affecting their business. Organizations that embrace an agile mindset and empiricism to enhance the power of team-work are able to be more nimble and resilient in a rapidly changing, highly competitive world.

CALL TO ACTION

Consider these questions with your team:

- Are organizational policies or processes preventing the development of people and teams?
- Can the organization support (with time, money, or other resources) certain areas to facilitate growing a stronger team identity?

---

11. Nexus is an approach for scaling Scrum for multiple teams working on the same product. For more information, see https://www.scrum.org/resources/scaling-scrum.

- How does the organization—specifically your leadership and stakeholders—respond to transparent information when the update is perceived as positive? When it is perceived as negative?

- In what ways can you help the organization embrace change and adaptability as a competitive advantage?

- In what ways does the organization leverage empiricism and focus on valuable outcomes in its processes and policies (e.g., budgeting)?

- Which challenges are hurting the most right now? Identify one or two experiments to help leverage the organization for Scrum Team improvement. For each experiment, be sure to identify the desired impacts and how you will measure them.

CONCLUSION AND WHAT'S NEXT

By now, you should understand that Scrum is a lightweight framework that is simple, yet powerful when put into action by a skilled, cohesive, self-organized team that embodies the Scrum values and embraces empiricism.

In the course of the book, we have explored the Scrum Framework and many common challenges in applying it, along with ways to overcome these challenges. We have introduced seven key improvement areas for Professional Scrum as a way to help guide you toward achieving greater benefits with Scrum. Opportunities for reflection and action have been sprinkled throughout the book. We hope we have challenged you to improve your way of working and that we have given you new insights into ways that your organization can improve.

BUSINESS AGILITY REQUIRES EMERGENT SOLUTIONS

Throughout this book, we have explored an iterative and incremental approach to delivering value in a complex and uncertain world. To solve problems, ideally you will focus on a simple process: Try something, learn something, repeat. Build the solution in line with your growing collective understanding, responding to the changes as you see them coming.

Organizations want to enable business agility, not just to "do Scrum." Business agility means a quick enough return on investment (ROI), flexibility and control over investment decisions, and the ability to easily change direction when new opportunities or risks arise. Iterative and incremental approaches, by themselves, don't always achieve these valuable outcomes. The core of Scrum—an agile mindset, empiricism, and teamwork—provides the necessary foundation for realizing the benefits of this iterative and incremental approach.

By paying attention to feedback from the Scrum Team, the market, and stakeholders, organizations can reap valuable insights that help them continually improve their products and the processes being used to create those products. These feedback loops are driven by the three enablers of empiricism: transparency, inspection, and adaptation. Feedback, reinforced by the Scrum values, enables a learning culture that encourages experimentation and continuous improvement.

This learning culture permeates every aspect of how an organization delivers products, from early conversations around what could be a good idea (a hypothesis), to delivering each "Done" Increment. The organization continually refines both the product and its delivery approach as it pursues its vision for the product.

In Chapter 1, "Continuously Improving Your Scrum Practice," we introduced seven key areas that support improvement: an agile mindset, empiricism, teamwork, team process, team identity, product value, and organization. Through the course of this book, we have expanded on each of these key areas, showing how to use them to help a Scrum Team to improve.

Along the way, we hope you have learned some important lessons:

- *Without knowledgeable, skilled, and dedicated people, Scrum doesn't work.* Creating valuable solutions in a complex world requires teams composed of motivated people with many different kinds of knowledge, skills, and experiences. These teams need supportive space in which team members can collaborate to build creative solutions and learn from doing so.

- *Teams need help from the organization.* Teams live within organizations, and the culture of the organization will shape teams, either helping them expand or restricting their growth. When friction arises between a team and the organization, look for what is driving the conflict between who the team is and how the organization operates. Try to understand where and why there is a conflict between the agile values and principles and the behaviors exhibited in the organization.

- *Mindset shapes culture, and culture informs process.* Having a positive agile mindset will help shape the culture that facilitates maximizing the benefits of Scrum and being resilient in a complex and rapidly changing environment.

- *Mastering Scrum is a journey, not a destination.* Practice makes better, never perfect. The more you practice awareness (of yourself and those around you), reflect, and then act with intention, the better you will become at creatively and productively solving problems and delivering solutions of the highest possible value. Where you are going on this journey will certainly be changing as well, so stay open to the possibilities.

Regularly revisiting the assessment questions in Appendix A, "A Self-Assessment for Understanding Where You Are," will help you to look for ways you and your teams can improve. Ask yourself:

- What are you learning?
- What has changed?
- What risks or opportunities are presenting themselves?
- Where do you see common themes?
- What trends do you notice?

In a similar way that individual skills improve, the Scrum Team and organization can improve by seeking active experiments to grow and learn, and by responding to insights and changes at an increasingly rapid pace. Teams and organizations improve by developing the following assets:

- A ruthless focus on value
- A relentless focus on technical excellence and getting to "Done"
- A spirit of continuous improvement, always seeking "better"

Acknowledge your present situation and look for that smallest next step that will bring you the most value in moving toward your goal. Change is hard, and using a framework will guide the change to be more focused, disciplined, and effective. Being clear about the framework you are using and using it as intended will provide the best benefits.

CALL TO ACTION

At the end of each chapter, we have issued a "call to action" intended to keep you moving forward on your ongoing journey to maximize the benefits of Scrum. Your journey doesn't end here, at the end of this book; in fact, it is just beginning. Reflect on your key insights, the actions you have already taken, and the results you have observed from those actions. Focus first on building a strong team and on the fundamentals of empiricism, and then build from there based on feedback. With experience and practice, activities that were very hard at the beginning will become almost effortless.

Consider scheduling time on your calendar to regularly reflect on your learning, observations, and insights in your journey of Scrum mastery. As you do, consider how you will incorporate these learnings to better serve your Scrum Team and your organization (and perhaps beyond). Continually inspect your results and adapt your approach.

Scrum's power derives from its simplicity. As the world becomes more volatile, uncertain, and ambiguous, you will need Scrum's simplicity to navigate the world's increasing complexity. Leaders who embrace simplicity and empiricism enable their people, teams, and organizations to thrive and, in turn, deliver better solutions to the world's challenges. We encourage you to be part of the Scrum.org mission to improve the profession of product delivery. Let professionalism guide you.

We wish you the best on your own journey of learning and improvement.

Scrum on!

A Self-Assessment for Understanding Where You Are

Before you can improve, you need to know where you may be falling short of your goals. These questions will help you identify the pain points that hurt the most. These pain points are often the most visible for the most people, and they tend to be interrelated. They are often what is causing your team to feel pressure, anxiety, or apathy. Try to answer each question openly and objectively, and if you are not sure, consider how you can get more information.

Business Agility

Business agility and effective use of Scrum are directly connected. If you are "doing Scrum" but are not realizing the business agility outcomes you desire, you should consider how you are applying the Scrum Framework with an agile mindset. To determine how agile your business is, rate your degree of agreement with the following statements on a scale of 1–10 (1 = highly disagree, 10 = highly agree).

- Your organization is satisfied with your product's return on investment.
- You produce a "Done" (i.e., potentially releasable) Increment at least once every Sprint.

- Your customers are happy with the frequency with which they receive releases.
- Stakeholder and customer feedback are incorporated into the product to improve the value of the product.
- You validate assumptions about the value of the work that you are doing based on market, customer, or user feedback.
- You can deliver new product capabilities in an acceptable period of time.
- You can respond to new opportunities or risks in an acceptable amount of time.
- You understand, and have evidence to support, your customers' needs.
- You understand how your users or customers use the product, including which features they use.
- You understand current and trending market conditions for your product.
- Your customers feel that the level of quality of your product is high.
- You spend an acceptable ratio of your product investment on maintaining the product or fixing defects (versus new product capabilities).
- Your teams are very satisfied with their work.
- Your teams are very satisfied with their learning and growth opportunities.

EFFECTIVE EMPIRICISM WITH SCRUM

To determine how empirical you are, rate your degree of agreement with the following statements on a scale of 1–10 (1 = highly disagree, 10 = highly agree).

- **We have a Product Owner and ...**
  - We have a single Product Owner who is empowered to make decisions to maximize the value of the product.
  - The Product Owner regularly communicates a clear vision for the product.
  - The Product Owner has easy access to data to help her measure the impact of changes to the product.

- The Product Owner is knowledgeable about the product strategy and how it aligns with business objectives.
- The Product Owner actively seeks input from stakeholders and sets expectations with stakeholders.
- The Product Owner is available to help answer questions and guide the value created by the Development Team during the Sprint.
- The Product Owner is able to focus adequate time on understanding customer/user needs, establishing and communicating the product vision, and exploring new ways of delivering value.

- **We have a Scrum Team and ...**
  - The Scrum Team feels empowered to make changes to its processes and tools.
  - The Scrum Team actively seeks to reduce waste in its processes.

- **We do Sprint Planning and ...**
  - The entire Scrum Team fully participates and achieves the purpose within the time-box.
  - The Scrum Team creates a Sprint Goal that provides a clear purpose for doing the Sprint.
  - The Scrum Team is able to plan the Sprint efficiently and effectively with their knowledge and the information available in the Product Backlog.
  - At the end of a Sprint, it is clear whether we have met the Sprint Goal.

- **We do Sprints and ....**
  - The Sprint is one month or less, and the length of the Sprint remains consistent.
  - The Sprint is short enough to give the business the flexibility it needs to limit investment risk, get feedback to validate assumptions, and change direction frequently enough.
  - There is always a potentially releasable Increment that provides business value by the end of every Sprint.
  - The Scrum Team consistently meets its Sprint Goals.

- The Development Team learns more about the business needs every Sprint through collaboration with the Product Owner and other stakeholders.

- **We have an Increment and ...**
  - The definition of "Done" reflects a releasable product and is expanding over time to improve quality and completeness.
  - The Scrum Team does not cut quality under pressure to deliver more.
  - The Product Owner is never surprised by the Increment inspected in the Sprint Review.
  - Stakeholders are nearly always happy with the Increment shown in the Sprint Review; when they are not, the Product Owner responds by using the feedback to adapt the Product Backlog.

- **We have a Development Team and ...**
  - The Development Team members have autonomy over how they develop and deliver the Increment, and they feel empowered to make these decisions.
  - All members of the Development Team have a clear understanding of the definition of "Done."
  - The Development Team works to clarify and enhance the definition of "Done" to improve quality and completeness over time.

- **We have a Product Backlog and ...**
  - The Product Backlog is available and understandable to the Scrum Team and stakeholders.
  - The Product Backlog is an ordered list representing what is currently planned for the product.
  - The Product Backlog clearly identifies the value of each item.
  - The Product Backlog is frequently refined and updated as more information is learned through delivering the product and inspecting changes in the environment.
  - The Product Backlog is not simply a translation of other requirements documentation handed to the Scrum Team.

- The Product Backlog is not simply an ever-growing list of every customer/stakeholder request, but rather reflects a thoughtful response to customer needs and desired outcomes.

- **We have a Sprint Backlog and …**
  - The Sprint Backlog clearly communicates progress toward the Sprint Goal.
  - At least one actionable improvement from a previous Sprint Retrospective is included in the Sprint Backlog.
  - The Development Team frequently updates the Sprint Backlog to reflect new learnings as the work progresses.
  - There is rarely partially complete work at the end of a Sprint.

- **We have a Daily Scrum and …**
  - The entire Development Team fully participates and achieves the purpose within the time-box.
  - The Daily Scrum is a collaborative planning session facilitated by the Development Team.
  - By the end of the Daily Scrum, the Development Team understands the progress made toward the Sprint Goal, any impediments blocking or slowing progress, and the plan for the next 24 hours.
  - The Daily Scrum is not simply a status update, but actively facilitates collaboration to help improve the ability of the team to deliver value.

- **We have a Sprint Review and …**
  - The entire Scrum Team and invited stakeholders fully participate and achieve the purpose within the time-box.
  - Sprint Reviews are collaborative and generate helpful feedback about the Increment and the product direction.
  - All necessary stakeholders attend to provide relevant and useful feedback.
  - Stakeholders understand the value of empiricism when solving complex problems; they don't view Scrum as simply a way to do more work in less time.

- Stakeholders are concerned with having a releasable Increment that meets a business objective rather than whether all the forecasted Product Backlog items were completed, or whether all applicable procedures were followed.

- There is more emphasis on having a releaseable, high quality Increment that provides value than on completing everything that was planned in Sprint Planning.

- **We have a Sprint Retrospective and …**

  - The entire Scrum Team fully participates and achieves the purpose within the time-box.

  - Sprint Retrospectives include open and meaningful discussions about how the Scrum Team is working.

  - During the Sprint Retrospective, the Scrum Team identifies actionable improvements to implement in the next Sprint.

  - The Scrum Team implements the actionable commitments in a timely manner and assesses the impact.

- **We have a Scrum Master and …**

  - The Scrum Master ensures that the Scrum Team understands and adheres to the Scrum Framework while enabling and encouraging self-organization.

  - The Scrum Master embodies the Scrum values and empiricism.

  - The Scrum Master actively helps the Development Team make its work transparent.

  - The Scrum Master helps the Scrum Team embrace the Scrum values and empiricism.

  - The Scrum Master embodies agility to the organization and actively works to remove organizational impediments.

  - The Scrum Master understands the Scrum Team's health and is helping improve collaborative teamwork.

  - The Scrum Master causes changes to improve productivity and quality without undermining self-organization.

  - The Scrum Master acts as a servant-leader, measuring her own success by the growth of the team and the team's success in achieving the benefits of Scrum.

EFFECTIVE TEAMWORK WITH SCRUM

To determine the effectiveness of teamwork in your Scrum implementation, consider the level of applicability of the following statements, rating them on a scale of 1–10 (1 = highly disagree, 10 = highly agree).

- **Commitment and Focus**
  - We measure success based on achievement of shared goals and outcomes.
  - We hold each other accountable to commitments and quality standards.
  - We make value-driven, consensus-based decisions.
  - All team members support team decisions and plans of action.
  - All team members are willing to push themselves beyond their comfort zone.
  - We focus on one or two small things, get those done, and then move on to the next thing.

- **Openness and Courage**
  - All team members proactively help others on the team.
  - All team members proactively ask for help.
  - All team members quickly admit mistakes and seek solutions.
  - All team members are willing to share their ideas and perspectives.
  - We handle failure or setbacks by reflecting on what we learned and trying another approach.
  - We bring up issues and concerns proactively and directly.
  - We are able to adapt to unexpected change.
  - Team members challenge assumptions, both their own and those of the wider organization.

- **Respect**
  - All team members are capable of and willing to resolve conflicts respectfully and productively.
  - We frequently provide each other with constructive feedback for individual and team growth.

- All team members are open to hearing and considering different ideas and perspectives.
- We work to improve cross-functionality and grow business, technology, and process knowledge across the team.

ANALYSIS OF ASSESSMENT ANSWERS

Go back and look at your assessment answers. Now consider the current trends for each one:

- In which areas are you moving toward desired outcomes?
- In which areas are you stagnating?
- In which areas are you moving backward?

Now consider these questions:

- Does it feel as if you are just going through the motions? Or do you show up with heart, intention, and commitment?
- How much open and honest discussion is happening within the Scrum Team about the challenges and ideas for improvement?
- How much control do the Scrum Team members have over how they do the work to develop and deliver the product?
- How much support is management providing to remove organizational impediments?

COMMON MISCONCEPTIONS ABOUT SCRUM

SCRUM IS NOT A METHODOLOGY OR A GOVERNANCE PROCESS

A methodology is "a body of methods, rules, and postulates employed by a discipline; a particular procedure or set of procedures."[1] A methodology does not work in a complex and unpredictable domain because it relies on knowing the solution and the steps that will get you there. In complex domains, teams must use an empirical approach to deliver value or solve problems. They must be able to determine their own processes and techniques and adapt them as they learn more through doing the work.

Scrum is a process framework that provides minimal boundaries, which enables self-organization while limiting risk. Everyone's implementation of Scrum will look different because each product and each team will have unique needs.

Many Scrum Teams work in organizations that care deeply about managing risk. They want to ensure that funds are being spent effectively and in alignment with business goals, that security and safety standards are being

---

1. By Permission. From Merriam-Webster.com © 2019 by Merriam-Webster, Inc. https://www.merriam-webster.com/dictionary/methodology.

met, and that they are not opening themselves to legal or regulatory liabilities. These organizations implement governance processes to try to control these risks.

Scrum is not a governance process, but it can help you control risk. Scrum can make waste in the organizational processes more transparent, which enables subsequent inspection and adaption to make these processes more effective. Scrum can help ensure alignment with business goals and provides opportunities to adapt early, bringing delivery back into alignment with business goals. When an organization focuses on defining the outcomes desired with regard to governance, risk, and compliance instead of defining the methods, it allows teams to meet those outcomes in the most effective way possible. By relentlessly focusing on building a "Done" Increment, the team simultaneously manages delivery risk.

SCRUM IS NOT A "SILVER BULLET" OR A WAY TO GET DEVELOPERS TO WORK FASTER

Simply "doing Scrum" will not fix your problems. People make Scrum effective; they develop creative solutions by making informed decisions based on empirical data. When people embody the Scrum values, the things that are holding them back become more visible. And when things are visible, there is a chance at improvement. Scrum done well is like a spotlight shining on your organization and the way you work—the good and the bad.

Using Scrum will likely create efficiencies in the development process, meaning some activities will take less time because of its emphasis on continuous improvement. But that misses the point of Scrum. Scrum's focus is on frequent delivery of value. Scrum is about working differently so that valuable pieces of the product can be released more frequently.

Delivering more of the wrong stuff faster is not very effective. You must be effective in determining what is valuable. You must be effective in adapting to feedback, empirical measurements of real value, and changes in the market.

You must be effective at getting to "Done." Scrum helps you achieve this level of effectiveness.

When it comes to product delivery, we choose effective over efficient. Efficiency is a secondary benefit of Scrum, and Development Teams will determine where they have opportunities to improve efficiency in their own processes. The key is to apply the transparency obtained from having a "Done" Increment to validate the value. The ability to achieve a "Done" Increment and unlock the flow of value is a natural benefit of the framework.

THE PRODUCT OWNER'S MAIN FOCUS IS NOT DOCUMENTATION OF REQUIREMENTS

A Product Owner's accountability focuses on maximizing the value of the product. This encompasses so much more than just writing requirements. A Product Owner works with stakeholders to understand their needs and set expectations. A Product Owner communicates the vision for a product in alignment with the business strategy and the organization's mission. A Product Owner makes difficult decisions about competing priorities and desires. A Product Owner needs to understand users and how they are using the product.

While the Product Owner is accountable for what is in the Product Backlog and the order (prioritization) of those items, she is likely to delegate some (or most) of the details.

THE PRODUCT BACKLOG IS NOT AN AGILE VERSION OF A TRADITIONAL REQUIREMENTS DOCUMENT

With Scrum, the organization focuses on delivering opportunistic pieces of valuable functionality.

The Product Backlog is a representation of product requirements and is open to change at all times, and it should evolve as the team learns more about the product through delivering Increments of the product. It should evolve as the team learns more about the users, as the team learns about changes in the market, and as business needs change. Even during a Sprint, the Product Backlog items may change as the team clarifies and confirms a common understanding through the process of building it.

The Product Backlog is not handed to a Scrum Team when they start an initiative. Likewise, it should not be treated as a contract that prevents collaborative negotiation and an openness to change.

THE PRODUCT BACKLOG IS NOT A LIST OF ALL REQUESTS

The Product Backlog provides transparency into what is planned in the product right now. The Product Owner is accountable for optimizing value, which is done through ordering of the Product Backlog. If the Product Backlog includes items that you don't intend to implement because they have low value or are not in alignment with the direction of the product, then you are obscuring transparency.

Every request should not be added to the Product Backlog simply to make stakeholders feel good that their request has been captured. A Product Owner fulfills her accountability by making the tough decisions about what will be done in regard to the product. A Product Owner may choose to say, "not now." If that item becomes relevant in the future, it will come up again and can be added to the Product Backlog at that time.

THE DAILY SCRUM IS NOT A STATUS MEETING

The Daily Scrum is a collaborative planning session to inspect progress toward the Sprint Goal and adapt the plan. It is not meant to account for how each person spent the previous workday. It is not meant to focus on individual status updates because that both loses sight of the Sprint Goal and inhibits the shared accountability of the Development Team to create a "Done" Increment.

The Daily Scrum is not meant to provide status updates to people outside the Development Team. Such a dynamic can cause a lack of transparency into progress and take away the emphasis on Development Team collaboration.

A Sprint Can Be Successful Even When All Planned Sprint Backlog Items Are Not Completed

Even within the shorter time frame of a Sprint, product delivery entails a great deal of complexity and unpredictability. The Sprint Backlog is not a promise to deliver a specific set of items within a specific timeframe. We recognize that we cannot perfectly plan, so we accept that ambiguity and make informed decisions to adapt our plan based on what we learn as the solution emerges. We use the Sprint Goal to provide focus and adapt the Sprint Backlog as we learn more.

A successful Sprint delivers a releasable product. A successful Sprint delivers value.

The Scrum Master Is Not Responsible for Tracking the Development Team's Work

The Development Team is self-organizing, which means the team members are responsible for monitoring their own progress and adapting their plan. A Scrum Master may support a Development Team by teaching them techniques to work more effectively together and to increase the transparency of their progress and outcomes.

The Sprint Review Is Not an Acceptance Meeting

The releasable Increment is already created when the team gets to the Sprint Review. The Sprint Review is an opportunity to gather feedback and collaborate on what to do next, but it does not lead to an accept or reject decision.

If stakeholders are not happy with the product they see at the Sprint Review, the Product Owner still makes the decision about how to adapt the Product Backlog. If a Product Owner is not happy with the product she sees at the Sprint Review, she should consider how to work more collaboratively with the Development Team during the Sprint to get the product she wants.

It Does Not Take a Lot of Preparation to Start Sprinting

A Scrum Team can start a Sprint if it has a Product Owner with a product vision, a Development Team with all of the skills to create a "Done" Increment, and a Scrum Master. Product Backlog refinement happens along the way.

Of course, it is helpful to have some startup activities such as training and lightweight process definition (e.g., creating a definition of "Done").

This is also probably a good time to clarify that there is no such thing as sprint 0, infrastructure sprints, or design sprints. The purpose of a Sprint is to produce a "Done" Increment. If you do not plan to produce a "Done" Increment, you are not doing a Sprint. Do whatever you feel is necessary to prepare to start (within reason—don't get caught in analysis paralysis!). Just don't call that preparation time sprint 0.

INDEX

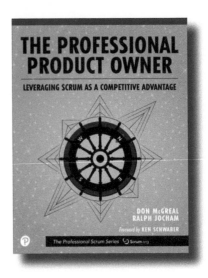

Photo by marvent/Shutterstock

VIDEO TRAINING FOR THE **IT PROFESSIONAL**

LEARN QUICKLY
Learn a new technology in just hours. Video training can teach more in less time, and material is generally easier to absorb and remember.

WATCH AND LEARN
Instructors demonstrate concepts so you see technology in action.

TEST YOURSELF
Our Complete Video Courses offer self-assessment quizzes throughout.

CONVENIENT
Most videos are streaming with an option to download lessons for offline viewing.

Learn more, browse our store, and watch free, sample lessons at
informit.com/video

Save 50%* off the list price of video courses with discount code **VIDBOB**

the trusted technology learning source

Photo by izusek/gettyimages

Register Your Product at informit.com/register

Access additional benefits and **save 35%** on your next purchase

- Automatically receive a coupon for 35% off your next purchase, valid for 30 days. Look for your code in your InformIT cart or the Manage Codes section of your account page.

- Download available product updates.

- Access bonus material if available.*

- Check the box to hear from us and receive exclusive offers on new editions and related products.

*Registration benefits vary by product. Benefits will be listed on your account page under Registered Products.

InformIT.com—The Trusted Technology Learning Source

InformIT is the online home of information technology brands at Pearson, the world's foremost education company. At InformIT.com, you can:

- Shop our books, eBooks, software, and video training
- Take advantage of our special offers and promotions (informit.com/promotions)
- Sign up for special offers and content newsletter (informit.com/newsletters)
- Access thousands of free chapters and video lessons

Connect with InformIT—Visit informit.com/community

the trusted technology learning source

Addison-Wesley • Adobe Press • Cisco Press • Microsoft Press • Pearson IT Certification • Que • Sams • Peachpit Press

 Pearson